NEW DIRECTIONS FOR INSTITUTIONAL RESEARCH

Patrick T. Terenzini, *The Pennsylvania State University*
EDITOR-IN-CHIEF

Ellen Earle Chaffee, *North Dakota University System*
ASSOCIATE EDITOR

Studying Diversity in Higher Education

Daryl G. Smith
Claremont Graduate School

Lisa E. Wolf
Claremont Graduate School

Thomas Levitan
University of South Florida/New College

EDITORS

NUMBER 81, SPRING 1994

JOSSEY-BASS PUBLISHERS
San Francisco

CONTENTS

An overview of themes and issues that emerge when addressing the study of diversity, reflecting the complexity and the opportunities for the institutional researcher.

Introduction to Studying Diversity: Lessons from the Field

Daryl G. Smith, Lisa E. Wolf, Thomas Levitan

For years now, higher education has confronted the challenges of diversity. While earlier formulations focused mostly on issues of access and preparation, diversity issues have broadened to include questions concerning pedagogy, the curriculum, notions of community, retention, decision making, faculty composition and evaluation, leadership, the role of staff, funding resources, and fundamental questions concerning institutional mission. In the past students were the focus, but now all constituents are part of the discussion.

At the same time, society is calling on higher education for transformation often associated with a different set of imperatives: excellence, accountability, and achievement.

On the face of it, the imperatives of diversity, associated with the changing demographics of our society and the realities of increasing global linkages, and the imperatives of excellence and accountability appear to be in tension. To some, focusing on diversity is in conflict with concerns about excellence. In reality, however, they are quite compatible and indeed fundamentally connected. This volume, focusing on the study of diversity, will reflect the significant relationship between educating successfully in today's society and educational excellence and, in particular, will highlight the ways in which education related to diversity requires fundamental transformations in educational values and practices—transformations that not only facilitate the success of students from diverse backgrounds, but the success of all students.

For the institutional researcher and others interested in studying diversity, the challenge is significant. Studying diversity no longer means simply developing a demographic census of who is in attendance. Moreover, the study of diversity cannot be removed from the ongoing controversies, challenges, and opportunities present on campus. Indeed, this monograph argues that the function of institutional research will be central to facilitating the campus dialogue on diversity. If it is true that issues relating to diversity require fundamental transformations in higher education, then studying diversity will also require rethinking the assessment and research process. A number of lessons can be learned from the study of diversity nationally and from the authors who have contributed to this volume.

Lesson 1. Research Matters: The Researcher Is Part of the Change Process

"Classical" metaphors of research suggest images of the distanced researcher removed from the questions being studied, attempting to develop an objective form of truth. This truth should inform institutional practice and policies, but more often than not the research is ignored. What is very clear is that the research questions asked and the methods used to answer them reflect the perspectives of those involved. Academic researchers as well as applied researchers have come to recognize that the questions asked, the methods used, and the analyses performed reflect perspectives that are not neutral and that must be acknowledged.

Moreover, it is clear that the very act of doing research on issues related to diversity begins a process of change. The results of surveys, interviews, and even the announcement of campus climate studies bring issues of diversity to the fore, and engender concern about who is doing the research, how it will be conducted, and how the results will be used. Even the discussion of who is to be included under the rubric of the term *diversity* often prompts a discussion of institutional priorities and issues. Is the study to deal primarily with racial and ethnic concerns, gender concerns, gay and lesbian concerns? This discussion phase by itself requires careful thought and planning.

One of the primary lessons to be learned is that studying diversity requires a commitment of time and energy and a recognition that important and complex issues will be raised that cannot be avoided. Research matters! The results of research can matter. Designing research to facilitate institutional decision making will be complex, will involve a variety of perspectives, and will require more preparation than has often been the case.

Lesson 2. Framing the Question: Focus on the Institution

What would our institutions look like and how would they function if we were educating a diverse group of students for a pluralistic society? This is the key question facing our institutions. To answer this question adequately requires that institutional research be conducted from the point of view of institutional, not individual, transformation. In the past, studies of diversity involved primarily an analysis of the background characteristics of students, faculty, and staff. The focus of the analysis was on the needs of and, in many cases, the deficiencies of, specific groups.

Today's institutional research must focus on the study of institutional success; institutional impact; institutional responses to the needs of faculty, staff and students; and institutional climate. This reframing is essential because it affects the perspective brought to the issues. If the student graduation rate is studied from the perspective of student background, the focus will be on such topics as academic preparation, gender, and race/ethnicity as factors in student success. If, however, the graduation rate is studied from the perspective of institutional success and accountability, the focus will be on the ways students are taught, issues of faculty–student interaction, institutional support for advising and teaching, the campus climate, and expectations for success. The data (for example, student graduation rates) might be the same, but the questions, the analysis, and the conclusions generated will be quite different. The way a problem is framed directly influences the types of strategies used to solve it. An assessment program that attends to the institution and the community as well as to the characteristics of the constituents will be an important element in studying diversity.

The study of diversity is embedded in issues of institutional quality. Institutions that do not successfully educate and graduate students from diverse backgrounds can no longer be considered successful. In contrast to days when a high drop-out rate might have been considered the sign of a highly competitive institution, today a high attrition rate must be considered a sign of institutional failure.

Lesson 3. Multiple Perspectives from Multiple Methods: The Power of Voice

The studies of diversity described in many of the following chapters reflect the ways in which the use of multiple methodologies is becoming common and necessary. Rather than relying simply on statistical analysis derived from empirical approaches such as archival and survey data, campuses are combining these approaches with a wide variety of qualitative approaches such as interviews, focus groups, and personal stories. Hearing the voices of individuals and attending to their experiences of the institution has a validity not represented by group means. Combined with aggregated data that reflect patterns within the institution, these "voices" add power and substance to the research. Moreover, in promoting change, campuses find that these voices are harder to dismiss and to ignore than tables and statistics concerning the campus climate or other issues.

The use of qualitative approaches also helps address one of the significant problems in research on diversity today: how to or whether to aggregate groups.

Quantitative approaches require a certain N to perform a variety of analyses. It is common to read reports indicating that there were not enough of some group and thus that group was eliminated. Alternatively, aggregating across groups is commonly done to resolve this issue or to simplify analysis. Latinos—whether Chicanos, Puerto Ricanos, or Cubanos—are all lumped together. Most problematic are studies that lump all the participants into one of two categories: white or nonwhite. The reality is that the experiences within Asian American and Latino groupings are important to acknowledge, yet our traditional methodologies make this very difficult. In addition, groups disaggregated by both gender and race/ethnicity are rarely considered. Because qualitative methods do not set limits for size, the approach can acknowledge the experiences of individuals and small groups and allow for hearing a diversity of perspectives that quantitative methods traditionally overlook. In particular, as Bensimon notes, "viewing the institution from the lives of those who are on the margin expands the unidimensional and partial story of those situated in the center and provokes a different understanding of their own situation as well as of the situation they create for others" (1992, p. 12). Qualitative and quantitative approaches used together can provide powerful insights into issues of diversity.

Lesson 4. Diversity Touches All Constituents and All Elements of the Institution: Dealing with Breadth and Staying Manageable

No matter where a study of diversity begins, whether analyzing graduation rates, the campus climate, or faculty hiring, the process of discussion and analysis inevitably leads to almost every other dimension: curriculum, campus responses to harassment, staffing, teaching, community, and so on. The interconnections among all these issues reflect the ways in which diversity touches all aspects of institutional life. The end result is that studying diversity can be difficult to manage.

Numerous strategies for keeping studies more manageable and yet appropriately broad involve technologies that allow issues of prominence to emerge. Qualitative and open-ended techniques permit important issues to emerge without the research team prejudging what these issues are. Campus climate studies and institutional satisfaction studies typically permit the articulation of a wide variety of issues within a manageable methodology. Some campuses also find it useful to study a particular dimension of diversity issues (such as the curriculum) but allow the conclusions to touch on a broader range of issues. It is also possible to design the research in stages so as to study one set of issues at a time. For example, some campuses have focused on race and ethnicity before gender issues, reflecting the desire to study one dimension of diversity in depth. But separating the study of racial and ethnic issues from the study of gender issues may not always be politically possible.

Lesson 5. Communication and Process Are Essential: From Language to Design

In the world of the institutional researcher, it is common to be given a topic to study and to generate relevant data within a short period of time. More than on most topics, issues of communication and design are fundamental to the research project related to diversity. Indeed, it would not be an exaggeration to say that the researcher puts himself or herself at risk by taking on a study of diversity without extensively consulting with and involving others. From the early decisions about language and how groups are to be named to the study design, multiple and important perspectives must be addressed. This reality presents both a challenge and an opportunity.

The challenge is that research on diversity is almost always politically and emotionally charged. Research on diversity is by its nature sensitive, prone to undetected bias, and open to multiple interpretations. The results of the study matter to those involved more than the results of most studies conducted in our institutions, and the results may lead to consequences that also matter. Moreover, studies of diversity directly involve multiple constituencies—students, faculty, staff, trustees, the community—in ways that few other topics do. Generating a study of graduation rates by race/ethnicity matters. How it is interpreted matters. What the consequences will be for members of those groups matters. The degree to which the results legitimate or challenge stereotypes matters.

A related challenge lies in having to engage directly the kinds of anger and alienation often found on campuses related to this topic. Indeed, one of the skills researchers must have is the capacity to recognize and be able to deal with the deep emotional underpinnings of research on topics of diversity. Campus communities and their researchers must engage issues that engender powerful anger and alienation—hardly a skill that colleges have developed.

Nevertheless, studying diversity presents an opportunity for the institution to evaluate how it is doing and to generate visions about the process of educating diverse students for a diverse society. It also creates an opportunity for the office of institutional research to be part of an important process of asking questions, designing studies, and formulating the results. Researchers for years have decried the ways in which their studies are marginal to institutional decision making and policy. In areas related to diversity, studies can be and have been central to decision making.

The key lesson, however, is that the process must be inclusive, and a diverse set of perspectives must be involved in questions from design to analysis and interpretation. Indeed, one of the very concrete lessons from the field is the beneficial use of research teams and an advisory committee at all stages from conception to report and discussion of meanings and implementation of results.

This Volume

It will become clear from reading the chapters in this volume that studying diversity extends far beyond "simple" methodological considerations. Rather, the goal of the volume is to provide some understanding of the deeply embedded issues facing institutional researchers, some reflections on the context for the study of diversity, some suggestions related to larger methodological issues, and some resources that might be useful.

Issues of transformation and quality are recurring themes in this volume. Yolanda T. Moses's chapter challenges underlying assumptions that diversity and quality are antithetical notions and outlines ways in which diversity and quality are deeply connected. While this approach could be seen as somewhat removed from the central concerns of research, it is important to understand how some of the historical analyses of diversity, suggesting that diversity and quality were in conflict, rested on the ways diversity and quality were assessed. For example, if SATs are a primary measure of student quality, then admitting women could be seen as lowering standards because of their lower average performance on the SAT. The contradiction here becomes evident if one looks at actual performance in college: women perform on average better than men. If the predictive validity of the SAT has a gender bias, then using it as a measure of quality biases the discussion of excellence. Thus, the issue of quality and diversity moves quickly from a conceptual issue to a question of assessment and measurement. Conversely, the role of education for leadership, citizenship, and performance in today's society suggests that effective engagement of diversity can be seen as an essential criterion for higher education in the same way that introducing technology to our campuses was seen as an essential component of educational practice and quality just a few years ago.

Antonia Darder's chapter suggests different institutional models for diversity and argues that a culturally democratic model best envisions what our institutions would look like if we were educating students for a diverse society. Moreover, the chapter reflects on the important role institutional research can play—for good or for ill—in each of the models presented. By emphasizing a different paradigm for the role of the institutional researcher, she emphasizes how research shapes the direction of the institution by the nature of the questions asked and the analyses applied. In this chapter the powerful energy and emotion that studies of diversity can provoke become clear. Darder's analysis is anything but dispassionate, and it requires the reader to understand the depth and levels of frustration that exist within higher education about the historically damaging role that research of all kinds has played in perpetuating racism, sexism, and homophobia. The chapter underscores the important ways in which the study of diversity engages issues of social justice along with educational quality. The language in this chapter is strong and the message is a powerful one. Researchers who have not been exposed to that perspective will find it provides important insights that support some of the ways the study of diversity becomes emotional and charged. Indeed, the capacity to deal with emotion and anger becomes an important skill for the researcher.

Henry T. Ingle's chapter and Penny Edgert's chapter provide alternative approaches to the study of diversity in ways that address the requirements of inclusivity and manageability. Ingle's chapter describes a portfolio approach to assessing diversity, allowing for the inclusion of multiple perspectives at all stages and providing opportunities for the inclusion of a variety of methods from archival to qualitative to more traditional quantitative information. Ingle also focuses on the ways in which campuses might develop processes to interpret and make use of the information gathered. Edgert describes a number of approaches being used on campuses to study campus climate—a rubric that acknowledges the different ways in which individuals and groups experience a campus and allows for looking at many aspects of the institution.

Marsha J. Hirano-Nakanishi's chapter, while focusing on some of the more traditional methodological issues facing researchers as they study campus diversity (such as standardized tests and categorization of individuals and groups), also reflects on the ways research on this topic can and should be understood in the context of institutional quality. By embedding her discussion of diversity in the literature on Total Quality Management, she highlights the ways that excellence and diversity are connected and frames the discussion in ways that point to institutional practice and performance.

The concluding resource chapter, written by Thomas Levitan and Lisa E. Wolf, provides an annotated list of institutional approaches, clearinghouses, books, and electronic mail resources. One of the ways in which the study of diversity can be kept manageable is by learning from and using models, instruments, and processes developed in other places. Few institutions have the resources that Stanford and the University of California at Berkeley used to design and carry out their major reports on diversity. Nevertheless, their studies are available and can be used and modified by institutions attempting to approach diversity in similar ways. This chapter lists many such resources with names of individuals and offices willing to be contacted.

Daryl G. Smith
Thomas Levitan
Lisa E. Wolf
Editors

Reference

Bensimon, E. M. *Redesigning Collegiate Leadership: Teams and Teamwork in Higher Education.* Baltimore: Johns Hopkins University Press, 1993.

DARYL G. SMITH *is associate professor of education and psychology at the Claremont Graduate School. She is author of* The Challenge of Diversity: Involvement or Alienation in the Academy.

LISA E. WOLF *is completing her doctorate in higher education at the Claremont Graduate School and is the residence life coordinator at Scripps College.*

THOMAS LEVITAN *is currently director of student affairs at the University of South Florida–Sarasota/New College and a doctoral student in higher education at the Claremont Graduate School.*

Diversity and excellence are connected in deep and complex ways and are discussed in relation to assessment, curriculum, teaching, and leadership.

Quality, Excellence, and Diversity

Yolanda T. Moses

Institutions of higher education in the United States have the opportunity to enjoy exciting and challenging transformations prompted by the issue of diversity. I use the word *transformation* rather than *reform* because the kinds of changes that are necessary require rethinking everything that we do within the structure, culture, and value system of our colleges and universities. The purpose of this chapter is to explore diversity as it relates to issues of quality and excellence. Because institutional researchers are often asked to develop methods to "assess excellence," a consciousness about the ways in which definitions, concepts, and measurements of excellence relate to issues of diversity needs to be developed. Diversity and excellence are discussed in this chapter as they relate to leadership, faculty and curricular excellence, and student success. Methods and techniques are proposed by which institutions can begin to assess the degree to which they are meeting the challenges of institutional transformation for diversity in a context of educational excellence.

Diversity Is Our Destiny

For the past two decades the changing demographics of American society have been increasingly reflected in our institutions of higher education. The civil rights movement and the second wave of the women's movement in the 1960s both advocated access to universities and colleges and curriculum inclusion as a part of their calls for social and political change. This continuing call *for* and response *to* equal access to higher education stems from demographic, social justice, economic, and social imperative pressures. Our nation's changing demographics tell us that by the year 2000, 85 percent of our new work force will consist of white women, people of color (both male and female), and

NEW DIRECTIONS FOR INSTITUTIONAL RESEARCH, no. 81, Spring 1994   © Jossey-Bass Publishers

recent immigrants. Many of these people are also first-generation college students (U.S. Department of Education, 1987; Wright, 1987; Green, 1988; Thompson and Roberts, 1985; Smith, 1989). Our nation's leading economists and business leaders tell us that the access of a more diverse population to higher education, and thus to professional occupations and middle-class status, is a necessary condition for the continued success of the American economy at home and abroad (U.S. Department of Education, 1987). Thus, in contrast to those who have described diversity and quality as antithetical (Bloom, 1987; Hirsch, 1987; Cheney, 1992), I believe that a truly excellent institution must be successful in educating the broad spectrum of its students and preparing students for participation in the society.

Preparing students for the world in which they live and work has long been the role of American colleges and universities. In today's world, which requires greater knowledge about diversity and the capacity to interact with persons from diverse backgrounds, educating students to live in a diverse world should be part of the mission of most institutions. All students, regardless of their backgrounds, certainly need to function and to thrive. Indeed, there are those who view diversity not as a new call for the education of new populations, but as a reaffirmation of the long-standing intellectual tradition that all students should be educated to be citizens of the world, and not just members of their local communities (Wong, 1992). In fact, preparing students to live and participate meaningfully in a diverse world, both locally and globally, is one of the new imperatives, and thus an important indicator of educational quality (Gaudiani, 1991; Smith, 1989).

Until recently, simply reaching out to and recruiting diverse students (as well as faculty, staff, and administrators) was seen as the primary goal of diversity efforts. Literature dating from the middle of the decade to today shows that while students from diverse backgrounds were admitted to universities and colleges, they were expected to do all of the adjusting to be successful in the institution, and not the other way around. For example, students of color were expected to fit in at predominately white universities with the assumption that the university went on with "business as usual" and that these students would be successful. Part-time students and older adult students were expected to fit in at traditional residential campuses that made no effort to accommodate their special needs (Thompson and Roberts, 1985; Smith, 1989; Richardson and De Los Santos, 1988). The implicit or explicit assumption has been that when minority group or other nontraditional students did not succeed it was somehow their own fault.

A paradigm shift is needed for how leaders and educators conceptualize, institutionalize, and measure excellence and in how excellence is *assured* for different groups of students. If higher education is to succeed in facing this challenge, it must rethink what it means to be an educated person in a culturally diverse world; it must take responsibility for assessing the excellence of its graduates; and it must structure the total learning environment of our campuses to reflect that commitment. Questions must be asked about how our staff and faculty reflect their diversity commitment in the curriculum, in cocurricular activities, in faculty–student relations, in student–staff relations, and in student–student (faculty–faculty, staff–staff) relations. How do we know we are succeeding? We must expand existing notions of quality and excellence, as well as develop new ways to measure effectiveness in the new diversity paradigm.

The enrollment of older students, students of color (both male and female), part-time students, economically poor students, differently abled students, gay and lesbian students, international students, and first-generation college-going students is having a profound impact on what is happening in our institutions because we are being asked to rethink and re-evaluate every dimension of institutional life, a process that in the long run has the potential to improve educational practice for all students (Wright, 1987).

Quality and Diversity

The conflict and opposition between quality and diversity is a false one. According to key national campus leaders, higher education associations, and researchers, in order for institutions to be of high quality, they must use diversity criteria as part of their definition of excellence (Karamcheti and Lemert, 1991). According to Donna Shalala, former chancellor of the University of Wisconsin, "[W]e cannot have first-class universities without diverse student bodies and staffs. We have got to convince faculty members that what is at stake is the quality of the university, that you can't have excellence without diversity. We have to make an educational argument, not a moral one. And if a large segment of the country does not have a first-class education, the health of the country is at stake" ("Ten Years After the Bakke Ruling," p. A16).

Following are some of the misconceptions that reinforce the notion that a diverse faculty, staff, and student population, especially a minority student population, has an adverse effect on institutional quality:

1. *Embracing diversity means lowering admission standards and therefore the overall quality of who is admitted.* The assumption here is that students of color, for example, are not as qualified to attend as white students. Data show, however, that the declining preparation of students is a national issue found in virtually all schools and among all students regardless of race (Smith, 1990).

2. *Standards for students are usually measured by standardized tests such as SAT scores and GRE scores, which have a high degree of predictive value: students who do not have high scores will be less successful.* Research shows that the predictive values of standardized tests are often poor, especially for women and minority students. That is, tests do not predict performance for those groups. Diverse achievement indicators such as grades, portfolios, junior year assessment, and capstone experiences are more appropriate predictors of success (Astin, 1993). Quality is multidimensional, not unidimensional. Institutions that are successful with diverse student bodies set high expectations and devise

evaluation approaches that truly reflect educational performance. They then proceed to support the efforts of students to achieve them (Minnich, 1991; Smith, 1989; Astin, 1982, 1993).

3. *Admissions policies are discriminatory in favor of diverse students, because there are "set asides" or special admission status for them.* Higher education institutions in the United States have always admitted students with different levels of preparation. "Quality" has always been presumed to embrace people with different strengths; whether they be geographical, athletic, or artistic (Smith, 1990).

4. *Minority and women faculty and staff hired into university slots to fill diversity or affirmative action quotas are not as qualified as faculty and staff hired through "normal" procedures.* If "normal" quality is measured by attendance at certain schools, publishing in only certain journals, or having narrow research interests that totally eclipse commitments to teaching and to student performance, then quality will always work against diversity. Remember, for many years gender and race were explicit factors limiting access to many prestigious institutions. Access to certain publications has been restricted by one's area of research and by one's gender. Moreover, diversity of perspectives and expertise is essential to educational programs. From that educational point of view, minority and women faculty bring quality, they do not dilute quality (Blackwell, 1987; Moses, 1989; Smith, 1989).

5. *The attempt to introduce issues of ethnicity, gender, and class into the university curriculum has weakened the curriculum. For example, the "real knowledge" in Western civilization courses is being shoved aside to make room for information about the contributions of people of color.* Some of the most exciting scholarship being done in traditional disciplines today is scholarship that discovers and integrates the voices of women and people of color who have long been excluded from the canon. This kind of research actually enhances the curriculum and provides another avenue by which students can be actively drawn into the learning process (Moses, 1989; Musil, 1992). Moreover, in most disciplines these new perspectives have added significant insights or informed traditional assumptions.

Assessment

Quality issues should focus on what the institution is doing to be responsive to the needs of its constituents. This requires colleges to commit to an examination of existing quality measures and to see if the measures support or hinder diversity initiatives. We need to develop indicators of success and quality that work.

With the growing interest in accountability and assessment issues, linking quality and diversity means that colleges and universities have an opportunity to establish public trust around an important issue. Bogue and Saunders

(1992) call these opportunities *partnerships of trust* between state and campus authorities based on a joint philosophy of quality.

Peter Ewell (1992) notes that if institutions are to create a climate where quality assurance can be guaranteed, then they must do the following: First, they must abandon their preoccupation with quality as a "thing" to be measured. With the assistance of those being assessed, we should develop more precise local definitions of the context in which evaluation takes place. Second, we should not see quality assurance as an add-on to the work that we do. Rather, we should be certain that data-gathering procedures are integrated and gather appropriate information for what is being measured. As Ewell wisely remarks, "If we take solving problems rather than running processes as our point of departure in quality assurance, we may be surprised at what we accomplish" (p. 47). Third, educational institutions should recognize that society has a legitimate interest in what they do. In the long run, institutions must listen to complaints from the "outside" in search of those that are legitimate, knowing that improvement is possible. Fourth, Ewell notes that quality is best assured at the level where the work is done. Processes such as accreditation and program review provide at best only a window into a wide variety of discrete and particular problems. As Ewell states, "The real job is to more fully understand what's happening in individual classrooms, laboratories, or support units, and how these settings work and don't work together" (p. 47).

Ewell and others conclude that assessment practice has moved from broad-scale, end-point testing toward such things as classroom research. We must understand how basic instructional operations, like placement and advising, actually work as opposed to how they appear in the catalog. These are some of the things to be analyzed if the goal is to improve educational excellence (Mentkowski, Astin, Ewell, and Moran, 1991).

This short discussion of quality and diversity reveals several ways in which issues of diversity and quality are tied together. The next section looks at diversity and quality at the institutional level, especially as they relate to students, faculty, the curriculum and pedagogy, and leadership.

Student Success and Diversity

What are the characteristics of student success, and how does this success relate to issues of institutional diversity? Does an institutional commitment to diversity lower the quality of the student experience?

For more than twenty years factors such as high school grade point average, socioeconomic status, SAT scores, and parental education were presumed to be important predictors of success (Astin, 1975; Tinto, 1987; Smith, 1990). In addition, noncognitive variables, such as good study habits, positive attitude toward college, self-confidence, understanding of racism, and campus involvement all help predict student success (Astin, 1975, 1982, 1993; Fields,

1988; Nettles, 1988). Tinto (1987) found that persistence rates are correlated not only to educational background, but to students' involvement on the college campus. Unfortunately, literature shows that older students, commuting students, part-time students, and students of color have demands on their time outside of the university that affect their persistence (Chacon, Cohen, and Strover, 1986; Smith, 1990; Astin, 1993; Moses, 1989).

Smith (1989) tells us that "underlying many of the discussions about the changing demographics and the needs of non-traditional student groups is the assumption that questions about access compete directly with questions of quality" (p. 89). Acknowledging that the higher education community must do something about the conflict of standards and excellence in higher education, she warns us not to assume that academic preparation is a problem solely of the nontraditional student: "It is often too quickly assumed that minority students are not prepared, that students with disabilities cannot learn, that part-time students are not committed and that alternative modes of learning are not legitimate" (p. 90).

The opposition of diversity and quality is a false one. While much of the evidence comes from the lower test scores of minorities and women on such standardized tests as the SAT or ACT, the predictive value and power of these tests is questionable (Smith, 1990). Astin (1993) does not denigrate the use of standardized multiple-choice tests in assessing student outcomes, but he warns us to remember their limitations: "They measure narrowly defined skills, and do not appear to be good indicators of student development in many important areas" (p. 429). The same thing can be said for learning assessment programs that rely on similar measures (Smith, 1989). The problem can be remedied by using multiple achievement indicators such as affective outcomes, portfolios, performance assessments, criterion-referenced measurement, and longitudinal assessment. Using multiple indicators does not require lowering standards for learning, only accepting alternate measures (Mentkowski, Astin, Ewell, and Moran, 1991; Smith, 1990).

Diversity in and of itself leads to institutional excellence. Astin (1993), for example, concluded that affirmative action initiatives and the promotion of multiculturalism on campus contributed positively to both the cognitive (intellectual) and affective growth of students. Students responded positively to diverse faculty, as well as to what they taught (multicultural courses or courses with multicultural issues imbedded in them). Students also noted positive cognitive and affective development if they participated in diversity activities: (1) taking a women's studies or ethnic studies course; (2) taking a world cultures course; (3) participating in racial and cultural awareness workshops; (4) discussing racial or ethnic issues; or (5) socializing with someone from another ethnic group (Astin, 1993).

In addition to the significant cognitive and affective growth in the whole area of "cultural awareness," students who responded positively to the diversity experiences also reported increased commitment to promoting racial understanding and increased satisfaction with their overall college experience. Exposure to diversity leads to intellectual as well as to social growth and maturation. Astin (1993) sums it up this way: "[T]here are many developmental benefits that accrue to students when institutions support an emphasis on multiculturalism and cultural diversity" (p. 430).

Faculty Role in Promoting Quality and Excellence

An important component of institutional excellence is the presence of a diverse faculty and their commitment and involvement. Smith (1989) lists five reasons: (1) diverse faculty provide support to students from diverse backgrounds; (2) the presence of diverse faculty and staff is a symbol to the diverse student body that the institution cares about them and the quality of interaction they have with campus personnel; (3) the presence of a diverse faculty and staff creates a more comfortable environment for students; (4) diversification of faculty and staff is likely to contribute a broader range to what is taught, how it is taught, and the development of opportunities for professional collaboration and the sharing of new ideas and approaches to traditional pedagogies; and (5) adequate numbers of diverse faculty and staff ensure that faculty play more than a token or symbolic role in institutional change (Smith, 1990).

It is not enough to hire people who are "the other." Retaining them and making them active members of the campus community is a sign of institutional quality (Moses, 1990). Research shows that historically underrepresented faculty are often treated as second-class citizens within departments that hire them as colleagues. They are perceived as "affirmative action" hires. Regarded as less qualified, they are isolated, ignored, and not taken seriously. Faculty and staff who are different are not promoted as rapidly as white males because they teach, advise, mentor students, and serve on university committees rather than do research or other more traditionally valued tasks (Moses, 1989). Reward structures continue to favor traditional indicators of quality, which put diverse faculty and staff at risk. If institutions are serious about faculty excellence, they must rethink the narrowly defined notion of excellence that currently guides most faculty tenure and promotion (and staff advancement) processes (Justus, Freitag, and Parker, 1987; Moses, 1991; Boyer, 1990; Span, 1988).

Another measure of institutional excellence is a faculty capable of creating and teaching a diverse curriculum. Institutions committed to educating all students for a complex multicultural society have as a crucial mission the creation of a curriculum that recognizes and engages diversity.

What should faculty be teaching in their diverse classrooms (as well as in the classrooms that should be diverse)? Ethnic studies and women's studies programs were created in the 1960s. Many students took advantage of these classes, but they were peripheral to the university curriculum. The environment of the 1990s demands that cultural diversity and multiculturalism issues be integrated into general studies, core, and major curricula. That is not to say that women's studies and ethnic studies programs should be abolished. They are still vitally important (Musil, 1992). Rather, faculty in these departments and programs must become part of the curriculum reform movements on campuses in traditional departments.

What kinds of content should be covered in the curriculum to assure faculty sensitivity to cultural diversity issues? Whatever the specifics, the curriculum should be guided by a set of values and principles reflecting the institution's mission and goals for diversity. Faculty should be a part of the leadership that develops the institutional vision. These goals should guide individual faculty in determining what is taught and how it is taught in their classrooms. I am arguing for a culturally diverse education on educational merits, not because it is "faddish." Faculty cannot be on the cutting edge of research in their disciplines unless they are dealing with the impact of the new scholarship in the classroom as well (Minnich, 1991; Musil, 1992; Takaki, 1988; Guy-Sheftall, 1991). Moreover, educating students for a diverse world requires knowledge about that world—knowledge that is scant in most traditional programs.

The institutional approach should not be one of coercion, but one of faculty development. Faculty should be provided incentives to attend conferences and workshops and to participate in curriculum integration projects. A faculty development approach allows faculty time to integrate diverse perspectives into what they already do. Curriculum integration projects that take a "value-added approach" for faculty have been quite successful (Musil, 1992; Schmitz, 1991; Guy-Sheftall, 1991; Minnich, 1991).

How faculty teach is just as important as what they teach in quality institutions (Astin, 1993). How the curriculum is delivered has tremendous impact on learning. Astin notes that the distribution of general education courses has little effect on the cognitive, psychological, and behavioral outcomes that lead to degree completion. Rather, it is how students approach general education, how the faculty delivers the curriculum, how actively the students are engaged and involved in the classroom discussion, and the extent to which students have meaningful interactions with peers and with faculty that really matters (Astin, 1993).

In light of this information, faculty should rethink the implementation of the general education curriculum. There is too much focus on form and content and not enough emphasis on pedagogy. Teaching techniques such as cooperative learning appear to yield more student satisfaction and higher achievement than traditionally competitive ways of interacting. Astin (1993) contends that students work harder when they know others will see their work, and that students are likely to learn more effectively when they in turn teach their peers.

Another interesting implication, tending to reinforce the institutional diversity commitment of putting student needs at the center of learning, is that students learn better if their classroom experiences are complimented or reinforced by experiences in other parts of the university such as student activities, housing, counseling, athletics, and student government. So, in addition to faculty, Astin (1993) advocates the involvement of student affairs personnel in the scope and development of general education programs.

This reaffirms what research in the area of retention of persons of color, women, and other diverse student groups tell us as well (Richardson and De Los Santos, 1988; Wright, 1987; Nettles, 1988). Recent research shows that students who are actively involved in the process of their own learning do well on cognitive as well as affective learning indices. Critical reasoning skills, understanding the coherence of the major, and how the major is connected to other bodies of knowledge are three key ingredients to all students' success in their majors. Volume 1 of the Association of American Colleges' (AAC) report (Schneider, 1991) contains a section on cultural diversity that encourages the engagement of students with diverse backgrounds in their majors as a way to engage them in the overall university experience.

Of the majors studied by AAC, women's studies was found to be the most student-centered. Musil (1992), in an analysis of seven women's studies programs, found that these programs link the intellectual and the experiential, creating personalized learning. These programs are intellectually challenging because they are built on a culture of trust and mutual respect within the classroom. In addition, Musil found women's studies classes to be participatory, experiential, diverse, and student-centered. Diversity is at the heart of the current intellectual agenda in women's studies; students expect to discuss difference in their classes and complain if this dimension is absent. These programs could be used as models by departments throughout the institution.

Diversity, Quality, and Leaders

The traditional hierarchical model of campus leadership is not effective in institutions with diverse students, faculty, and staff. While it is important for the president and the governing body to provide overall structural leadership, frame the questions, and set the tone for promoting institutional diversity, a cross section of campus community members must create comprehensive plans and develop ways to assess success—ways that enhance quality but not at the expense of diversity.

A variety of campus leaders from president to institutional researcher, from faculty member to student, can and must play a significant role in institutionalizing diversity.

Campus leaders at all levels, including faculty, staff, and students, must work together to articulate a clear vision of what their institution would look like if cultural diversity were part of the educational mission and if the institution were successful in enhancing diversity among students, faculty, staff, and governing body.

Campus leaders must develop consensus among various constituencies about the mission statement and diversity goals of the university.

Campus leaders must work with the general campus community to develop planning processes to implement the goals of the diversity plan.

Campus leaders must articulate a plan for measuring the success of diversity efforts.

Campus leaders must assure that adequate resources are available to implement and assess the diversity goals. Even in times of economic austerity, the resources for institutionalizing diversity must be part of the university-wide priority system.

Policies and procedures must be established to create a supportive and nurturing environment, including policies on sexual harassment, hate speech, physical accessibility, student grievance procedures, and faculty and staff development.

This comprehensive institutional approach empowers the president and other leaders at the top of the formal academic hierarchy as well as faculty, staff, and students to work toward a common vision of diversity in which diversity and quality are not antithetical. The commitment of leaders tells faculty, staff, and students that diversity is valued and important; the commitment of the various institutional constituents places pressure on leaders to develop and maintain programs and policies.

In summary, university leaders have the task of narrowing the gap between words and deeds, providing resources to carry out new initiatives, creating new ways of looking at excellence, and setting the tone for the discussion.

Conclusion

This chapter has explored the issue of diversity as it relates to issues of quality and excellence. I have looked at leadership and institutional quality, faculty and curricular excellence, and student success. While a few institutions of higher education may have achieved diversity in every aspect, most are still struggling to get there.

Areas of research in quality and diversity measurement still require attention. For example, while it may be ideal for students to attend college full-time, live in the dormitory, and work part-time on campus, there are a growing number of students who are older, who attend part-time, who commute, and who work full-time. These students deserve the same attention and research on how they learn and how institutions can provide optimum opportunities for them to grow and develop as is paid to traditional-age students. In summary, research shows that those institutions that encourage the hiring of diverse faculty and staff, promote diversity as an educational excellence issue, and reward faculty and staff for their efforts are institutions that have integrated quality and diversity issues. Programs that put students at the center of the teaching and learning process also score high on student satisfaction as well as on cognitive and affective skills acquisition. At the heart are the assumptions, often made through institutional research, about quality and diversity that drive these programmatic efforts.

References

Astin, A. W. *Preventing Students from Dropping Out.* San Francisco: Jossey-Bass, 1975.

Astin, A. W. *Minorities in Higher Education: Recent Trends, Current Prospects and Recommendations.* San Francisco: Jossey-Bass, 1982.

Astin, A. W. *What Matters in College: Four Critical Years Revisited.* San Francisco: Jossey-Bass, 1992.

Blackwell, J. E. *Mainstreaming Outsiders.* New York: General Hall, 1987.

Bloom, A. *The Closing of the American Mind.* New York: Simon & Schuster, 1987.

Bogue, G. E., and Saunders, R. L. *The Evidence for Quality: Strengthening the Tests of Academic and Administrative Effectiveness.* San Francisco: Jossey-Bass, 1992.

Boyer, E. *Campus Life: In Search of Community.* Princeton, N.J.: Carnegie Foundation for the Advancement of Teaching, 1990.

Chacon, M. A., Cohen, E. G., and Strover, S. "Chicanas and Chicanos: Barriers to Progress." In M. A. Olivas (ed.), *Latino College Students.* New York: Teachers College Press, 1986.

Cheney, L. V. *Telling the Truth: A Report on the State of the Humanities in Higher Education.* Washington, D.C.: National Endowment for the Humanities, 1992.

Ewell, P. T. "Feeling the Elephant: The Quest to Capture 'Quality.'" *Change,* 1992, 24 (5), 44–47.

Fields, C. "The Chicano Pipeline: Narrow, Leaking, and in Need of Repair." *Change,* 1988, 20 (3), 20–27.

Gaudiani, C. "In Pursuit of Global Civic Virtues: Multiculturalism in the Curriculum." *Liberal Education,* 1991, 77 (3), 12–15.

Green, M. F. *Minorities on Campus: A Handbook for Enhancing Diversity.* Washington, D.C.: American Council on Education, 1988.

Guy-Sheftall, B. "Practicing What You Preach: The Legacies of an Ex-English Teacher." *Liberal Education,* 1991, 77 (1), 27–29.

Hirsch, E. D. *Cultural Literacy: What Every American Needs to Know.* Boston: Houghton Mifflin, 1987.

Justus, J. B., Freitag, S. B., and Parker, L. L. *The University of California in the Twenty-first Century: Successful Approaches to Faculty Diversity.* Berkeley and Los Angeles: University of California Press, 1987.

Kamacheti, I., and Lemert, C. "From Silence to Silence: Political Correctness and Multicultural-ism." *Liberal Education,* 1991, 77 (4), 14–18.

Mentkowski, M., Astin, A. W., Ewell, P. T., and Moran, T. *Catching Theory Up with Practice: Conceptual Frameworks for Assessment.* Washington, D.C.: ASHE Assessment Forum/American Association of Higher Education, 1991.

Minnich, E. K. "Discussing Diversity." *Liberal Education,* 1991, 77 (1), 2–16.

Moses, Y. T. *Black Women in Academe: Issues and Strategies.* Washington, D.C.: American Association of Colleges, 1989.

Moses, Y. T. "The Challenge of Diversity: Anthropological Perspectives on University Culture." In *Cultural Diversity and American Education: Visions of the Future. Education and Urban Society,* 1990, 22 (4), 402–412. (Special edition.)

Moses, Y. T. *The Recruitment and Retention of Minority Faculty and Students. Women at the Helm: Pathfinding Presidents at American Colleges and Universities.* New York: University Press Association, 1991.

Musil, C. M. (ed). *The Courage to Question: Women's Studies and Student Learning.* Washington, D.C.: Association of American Colleges, 1992.

Nettles, M. *Toward Black Undergraduate Student Equality in American Higher Education.* Westport, Conn.: Greenwood Press, 1988.

Richardson, R., and De Los Santos, A. "From Access to Achievement. Fulfilling the Promise." *Review of Higher Education,* 1988, *11* (4), 323–328.

Schmitz, B. "Diversity and Collegiality in the Academy." *Liberal Education,* 1991, 77 (4), 19–22.

Schneider, C. G. "Engaging Cultural Legacies: A Multidimensional Endeavor." *Liberal Education,* 1991, 77 (4), 9–19.

Smith, D. G. *The Challenge of Diversity: A Question of Involvement or Alienation.* Washington, D.C.: American Association of Higher Education, 1989.

Smith, D. G. "Challenge of Diversity: Implications for Institutional Research." In M. T. Nettles (ed.), *The Effect of Assessment on Minority Student Participation.* New Directions for Institutional Research, no. 65. San Francisco: Jossey-Bass, 1990.

Span, J. *Achieving Faculty Diversity: A Sourcebook of Ideas and Success Stories.* Madison: University of Wisconsin System, 1988.

Takaki, R. *Strangers from a Different Shore: A History of Asian Americans.* Boston: Little, Brown, 1989.

"Ten Years After the Bakke Ruling." *Chronicle of Higher Education,* June 29, 1988, A16.

Thompson, I., and Roberts, A. (eds.). *The Road Retaken: Women Reenter the Academy.* New York: Modern Language Association of America, 1985.

Tinto, V. *Leaving College.* Chicago: University of Chicago Press, 1987.

U. S. Department of Education. *A Nation at Risk. The Imperative for Education.* Washington, D.C.: U.S. Department of Education, 1987.

Wong, F. "Diversity and Our Discontents." *AAHE Bulletin,* 1992, *45* (2), 1–3.

Wright, D. J. (ed.). *Responding to the Needs of Today's Minority Students.* New Directions for Student Services, no. 38. San Francisco: Jossey-Bass, 1987.

YOLANDA T. MOSES is professor of anthropology and president of City College of the City University of New York.

This chapter considers issues related to institutional research and its potential role in the move toward an ethos of cultural democracy in higher education.

Institutional Research as a Tool for Cultural Democracy

Antonia Darder

> [W]hen we notice that our social institutions are driven by the larger political contexts in which they are embedded, we are forced to acknowledge that the content of our research and the methods we use are likewise subject to the prevailing political forces.
>
> Kenwyn Smith (1990, p. 121)

American educational institutions are currently struggling to contend with the widespread demographic changes that are sweeping this country. As the population of people of color increases in the United States, it is becoming far more difficult to maintain the facade of cultural equality without dramatically increasing the number of students, faculty, and administrators of color on college and university campuses. Yet cultural equality is not only about numbers. It is, foremost, about an institution's ability to embrace a culturally democratic view of life that not only supports participation by all constituents, but also provides avenues for different cultural voices to be heard and integrated within the changing culture and history of the institution.

This struggle for cultural democracy[1] cannot be defined merely in terms of social justice paradigms that focus solely on the redistribution of material and nonmaterial benefits within the academy. Such a transformation must also address the ideological tenets and philosophical contradictions that have historically structured academic environments to benefit an elite group, while systematically marginalizing the participation of "the other"—people of color, women, gays and lesbians, and the working class (Young, 1990).

Most importantly, institutional change in the interest of cultural democracy cannot take place without major shifts in the manner in which school life is organized, academic issues are framed, education is actualized, and research is conducted (Smith, 1990; Crossen, 1988; Jaramillo, 1988; Loo and Rolison, 1986; Sanders, 1987). Although each of these areas of change is equally significant and vital, this chapter will specifically consider issues related to institutional research and its potential role in promoting an ethos of cultural democracy in higher education.

Institutional research, as a tool of traditional organizations, has often contributed to the perpetuation of asymmetrical power relations and the subordination of groups existing outside the mainstream. Inextricably linked to organizational values, beliefs, and practices defined by the structure of Western scientific thought, institutional research has served to make acceptable decontextualized and victim-blaming views of culturally diverse students—students who, more often than not, have found it difficult to succeed within the traditional structure of American higher education.

For example, test scores are widely used by college and university researchers to make conclusions about the future success of students of color. Their academic ability and potential are often determined by the scores they receive on standardized tests, even though these tests reflect the norms of the dominant culture and class. Moreover, the knowledge required to score well on such tests is generally achieved by means of the student's exposure to certain educational conditions. These conditions include the availability of well-prepared teachers, challenging instructional approaches, higher teacher expectations, adequate educational materials and equipment, and significant home educational resources—the very conditions that have been historically denied to the large majority of students from disenfranchised communities. Yet such differences in context are usually ignored; instead, students who score poorly on standardized tests are judged less able or less motivated, a practice that places the fault for lower scores directly on the student.

Institutional values and practices that sustain racism, sexism, classism, and homophobia in educational settings have perversely shaped and defined the nature of institutional governance, hiring practices, academic standards, testing and assessment, curriculum design, faculty–student interactions, financial priorities, and what is deemed legitimate research. As a consequence, traditional institutional research on diversity unwittingly supports institutional conditions that perpetuate:

- Simplistic perceptions of discrimination by failing to distinguish those acts of discrimination that function in the interest of exclusion and those that function in the interest of diversity
- A view of women and people of color as deficient
- An overemphasis on the "special" attributes of people of color to justify their entry into the institution

- Admitting too few people of color to enact an actual culture of diversity
- Insufficient services for promoting the success of disenfranchised students, faculty, and staff
- Hostility toward alternative cultural spheres that promote cultural integrity
- The silencing of discourse that fails to adhere to the Eurocentric ideal of dispassionate objectivity
- An absence of knowledge of students' histories and community realities
- The collusion of white students, white faculty, and white administration resistant to institutional change
- Fragmentation of subordinate group leadership to forestall institutional change
- Arguments of "political correctness" to abdicate social responsibility to struggle for equality
- Research-driven classifications (for example, "Hispanic" or "minority") that obscure the extent to which diversity actually exists within educational institutions.

Critique of Traditional Research Values

Educational conditions promoting inequality have been made possible by the underlying philosophical assumptions that inform traditional research methodology, namely, the acceptance of a dualistic, objective, value-free, hierarchical, and instrumental perspective regarding knowledge. It is a view that sees human beings as separate from nature, and thus as objectifiable, observable, quantifiable, predictable, and controllable. Through objectifying human beings into "things," human behavior can be treated as if it existed according to a predetermined set of universal rules, independent of the contexts in which the behavior takes place. Knowing the universal causes and effects provides the instrumental basis on which to effectively intervene and manipulate the flow of events, to bring about a desired control over the environment (Fay, 1987).

Traditional research has emerged from an authoritarian context bent on the prediction of the environment for the purpose of controlling and dominating its evolution, with an emphasis on the hierarchical categorization and compartmentalization of human experience. As a consequence, the belief exists that to conduct legitimate research, to produce legitimate knowledge, requires distancing "oneself emotionally from the rest of life" (Slater, 1991, p. 99). Both Philip Slater (1991) and Page Smith (1990) speak against this "rationalism of science."

> [T]he vaunted rationalism of science is often merely a guise for the zealous suppression of feeling which authoritarianism has always demanded.... The most irrational of all beliefs is the belief in rationalism...and the most subjective of all delusions is the belief that objectivity is possible. [Slater, 1991, p. 99]

[T]here is no such thing as "value-free" thought or research; those who act sincerely on such a premise deceive the world and, more dangerously, themselves.... The notion of value-free inquiry of social research without reference to social ends is the bugaboo of escapist science. [Smith, 1990, p. 161]

Other aspects of traditional educational research include a tendency toward reductionism, an overemphasis on the search for universals and homogeneity, and ethnocentric bias. These tendencies have resulted in the production of decontextualized knowledge, limiting the attention given to the unique impact of cultural, gender, and class influences in the attitudes and behaviors of students from subordinate cultures. Gordon, Miller, and Rollock (1990) perceive this neglect as "probably the result of androcentric, culturocentric, and ethnocentric chauvinism in Euro-American and male-dominated production of social science knowledge. We refer to this chauvinism as communicentric bias: The tendency to make one's own community the center of the universe and the conceptual frame that constrains all thought" [p. 15].

Research and Social Power

Without doubt, institutional relations of power are always at work in the manner in which traditional research is defined, implemented, and utilized within educational environments. In other words, the primary purpose of traditional research and the cultural values that inform it is directly related to the production of knowledge; and this knowledge is intimately linked to questions of social power. Michel Foucault (1977) describes this relationship between knowledge and power:

Truth is a thing of this world: it is produced only by virtue of multiple forms of constraints. And it induces regular effects of power. Each society [culture] has its regime of truth, its "general politics" of truth: that is, the types of discourse which it accepts and makes function as true; the mechanism and instances which enable one to distinguish true and false statements; the means by which each is sanctioned; *the techniques and procedures accorded value in the acquisition of truth; the status of those who are charged with saying what counts as true.* [p. 131; italics added]

The emphasis on objectivity and value-free knowledge can readily be understood from the standpoint of preserving the integrity of the status quo. It is generally those who are most protective of current conditions who most adamantly insist on institutional research that reflects a neutral and objective perspective, and who likewise respond with great suspicion to any research results that challenge the existing relations of power. Further, this emphasis on objective and value-free research functions to veil the implicit control the dominant culture holds over subordinate populations. Slater (1991) addresses this phenomenon and its consequences:

> It is easier for those who are satisfied with things as they are to appear neutral, unemotional, and unmotivated. The motivational impetus of those who seek change is more visible. They are more likely to be seen as "shrill" or "strident."... Those who seek change—those who attempt to challenge [explicitly] the powers that be—must speak louder in order to be heard at all, and the demand for a quieter, "more objective" voice is an effective way to silence them.... [And] when dissenting voices grow in numbers, authoritarian [institutions] will often stave off change by calling for further study. [p. 100]

Slater's comments point to the manner in which institutional research is used to prevent movement and to subvert institutional transformation. Instead of utilizing institutional resources for necessary organizational change, time, money, and human expertise are diverted to abstract research tasks that in and of themselves change nothing. It is as if change could somehow be pretended or magically actualized through the technocratic accumulation of volumes of "scientific" research reports. Frank Fisher (1985) describes the power of such "technocracy": "The power of technocracy is based on a positivistically oriented empirical conception of knowledge, which is reflected in a growing inventory of operational techniques such as cost-benefit analysis, operations research, systems analysis, strategic planning and computer simulations. Emphasizing the tenets of value-neutral objectivity, empirical operationalism and professional expertise, modern technocracy stands or falls with the ideology of scientism" [p. 232].

In summary, what is clearly missing in the traditional perspective concerning institutional research is an acknowledgment of the manner in which culture and power intersect to support a view of research that is apolitical and ahistorical. The standards and norms assigned and the approach utilized are encapsulated in a belief in the existence of universal values and an ideal of individualism and assimilation. These function to perpetuate a view of research that is not only devoid of critical[2] insight, but that reduces knowledge into abstract parts and perceives ideas as useful only to the extent that they produce actions that sustain the status quo. By so doing, traditional research reinforces the homogenizing intent of the dominant culture, while negating the cultural reality of subordinate groups; perpetuates a deficient view of women and people of color, while positioning the researcher as neutral and objective; denies the political nature of the research process, while assuming a moral posture of superiority; defines what constitutes legitimate knowledge, while ignoring the impact of sociopolitical contexts on such a value judgment; and de-emphasizes issues of social class and sexual orientation, while the hidden values reproduce social class inequality and compulsory heterosexuality.

Institutional Responses to Cultural Diversity

All educational institutions are fundamentally grounded on a set of values and beliefs that inform the manner in which they engage with questions of cultural diversity. All educational institutions enact an organizational culture that enhances or deters the process of cultural diversification. Institutional research on diversity must address the manner in which cultural democracy is stifled and truncated in the interest of preserving the existing organizational dynamics of power at work. Toward this end, it is valuable to assess the manner in which institutions respond to questions of cultural diversity. For purposes of discussion, most institutional responses to cultural differences can be considered in terms of an organizational power continuum that moves from traditional to culturally democratic, with liberal and multicultural reference points existing in between:

Traditional——Liberal——Multicultural——Culturally Democratic

In creating this framework, certain fundamental assumptions are clearly at work. First, culture incorporates all the implicit and explicit relationships and interactions that impart a sense of continuity and integrity to community life, despite individual differences. In as much as shared cultural beliefs, values, mores, and assumptions strongly shape individual and organizational practices and responses of a group, the environmental conditions in which groups live and work also impact their cultural practices and responses. Hence, efforts to contend with issues related to cultural differences in a reductionistic and decontextualized manner can easily lead to distortions of reality and major flaws in the subsequent prescription of institutional practices. Second, race, class, gender, and sexual orientation constitute subcategories of culture and thus represent differentiating systems of belief within the particular worldview. All cultural communities must contend with the underlying cultural assumptions that shape their prevailing views related to each of these dimensions of life. Third, racism, classism, sexism, and homophobia exist as interlocking spheres of institutional oppression that are driven by institutional practices (carried out by individuals) supporting what Iris Marion Young (1990) calls the "five faces of oppression": exploitation, marginalization, powerlessness, cultural invasion, and violence.

Also significant to the following analysis of institutional responses to diversity is a critical view of power. Such a view encompasses a notion of power as existing everywhere, forever at play when people come together. Thus, power is perceived as a social phenomenon that occurs between and among people—never in a vacuum. What institutions do, as much as what they do not do, affects the lives of their constituents, because institutions exercise power through decisions that lead to particular actions and consequences. Most importantly, power must be understood with respect to the impact that actions and their consequences have on particular groups. What are the consequences of institutional research, policies, practices, and standards? Who benefits the most from particular kinds of research, policies, practices, and standards? Who benefits the least? Whose voices are heard and whose participation is valued? These are useful questions for unveiling the power dynamics at work within an institution and identifying possibilities for creating the conditions for social justice and equality.

The remainder of this chapter will provide a framework to consider the manner in which four different institutional paradigms—here termed *traditional, liberal, multicultural,* and *culturally democratic*—engage the issues of cultural diversity and how they might inform institutional research.

The Traditional Institution

The values of the traditional institution support a view of culture as a depoliticized and neutral construct. In such an institution cultural differences, for the most part, are denied and are not considered legitimate. Hence, when cultural differences between people surface, much effort is made to label them as an individual phenomenon. Any effort to openly address cultural differences between groups is viewed as suspect, generating much talk and concern about divisiveness and tribalism. This response is supported by an ideology that reinforces the notion of American culture as a "melting pot" and a belief in cultural amalgamation, social Darwinism ("survival of the fittest"), and the doctrine of Manifest Destiny (an ostensibly benevolent policy of American imperialistic expansion).

The value system within a traditional organization places a great deal of emphasis on unity, conformity, and homogeneity, on the one hand, and on the ideal of individualism and a "boot-strap" mentality, on the other. To support the utmost possibility of unity, conformity, and homogeneity, power relations are highly centralized and marked by a strong hierarchical and authoritarian governance structure. This strong homogenizing effort results in positions of power being held almost exclusively by members of the dominant group. Little action, if any, is taken to address issues of diversity; these are generally ignored or dealt with in a manner that forces conformity. As a consequence, subordinate groups are generally excluded from participation and perceived as deficient, even to the point of being considered genetically inferior. Moreover, traditional institutions are marked by strong xenophobic attitudes regarding the use of languages other than English anyplace other than in the foreign language classroom.

The expressed purpose of research at traditional institutions is to produce "objective" knowledge that is focused upon prediction of conditions and subsequent interventions, with the goal of better managing or controlling the institutional environment through more effective control of its constituents. In the area of diversity, research is focused upon identifying deficits in subordinate groups and determining ways to facilitate widespread societal assimilation. This research is often found at work in vocational tracking of working-class students, women students, and students of color, particularly within the community college system, a practice that is considered to be the most effective educational approach to remediating problems caused by presumed poor academic achievement. Simultaneously, this approach meets the demands of the labor market. Generally, the underlying perspective here is that "diversity is viewed as deviance; and differences are viewed as deficits" (Gordon, Miller, and Rollock 1990, p. 15).

The Liberal Institution

Liberal institutions view culture as primarily an apolitical and decontextualized phenomenon that is readily identified as the experience of Latinos, African Americans, and other subordinate cultural groups. Cultural differences are considered to legitimately exist in the world, but their social importance is minimized or they are viewed as exotica. When cultural differences are addressed within such a context, the goal is to reveal the human similarities that unite all people. This approach is driven by an ideological foundation that is often described as "color-blind"—an ideology steeped in a belief in universalism, assimilation, and a notion that all human beings are essentially the same "under the skin."

Liberal, like traditional, institutions place an emphasis on unity and conformity by highlighting the similarities among people, and place an even greater emphasis on the uniqueness of the individual. Such values reinforce power relations that remain highly centralized, although they also lead to a more liberal hierarchical and authoritarian governance structure than is found at traditional institutions. As a consequence, those in middle management positions may gain more influence and control within the organization. Most of the positions of power are held by members of the dominant culture, but people of color are generally brought into the organization at entry or service levels. The belief that there are few people of color who are qualified for professional positions highlights discussions related to hiring, as does concern about finding the "right fit."

When the liberal organization chooses to address cultural differences, the extent of change is at a very basic content level, leading to the "adding-on" of cultural artifacts that are symbolic of diversity (for example, ethnic art on the walls, ethnic food in the cafeteria, and other forms of window dressing). People of color are both seen and treated with benevolence and are granted the possibility of becoming equal to members of the dominant culture, *if* they can overcome their cultural environments. Victim-blaming attitudes are often hidden beneath the organization's drive and passion to help the "disadvantaged and deprived." As a consequence, these attitudes support a missionary mentality. There is some acceptance of language diversity but, without question, English is considered the most important language.

The liberal institution must contend with oppositional responses to its liberalism from conservative members of the institution or the larger community. Opposition is generally most prominent among those who hold a strongly xenophobic and ethnocentric view of life in the United States. Most of their concerns are strongly linked to the need to be reassured that their own privileges and entitlements as members of the dominant culture will not be jeopardized.

Liberal institutional research strongly reflects most of the apolitical and ahistorical tenets of traditional research, with a similar emphasis on prediction and control of the environment. Much of the research on cultural diversity is focused on discovering the similarities and differences between the dominant and subordinate groups. The similarities are used by these institutions to promote an assimilationist ideal and efforts to integrate. Differences are studied primarily to identify areas that require intervention to assist students of color to perform as well as members of the dominant culture. There is some development of descriptive ethnographic approaches that function to generate popular narratives about subordinate groups.

The Multicultural Institution

The multicultural institution views culture as a legitimate and significant determinant of individual identity, but the focus remains on members of subordinate cultural groups. Cultural differences are generally acknowledged and a strong diversity rhetoric permeates the institutional discourse. Cultural differences are addressed in an effort to find ways to limit the increased tensions that result from an increasingly diverse institutional environment. The prevalent ideology within the multicultural institution is shaped by a belief in "fair and equal" representation and cultural pluralism.

The multicultural institution places a greater emphasis on shared common values, as the distribution of power begins to shift as an increasing number of members of subordinate groups enter the institution. As a consequence, the multicultural institution is marked by its greater decentralization of power and greater liberalizing of the traditional governance structures to accommodate differences. Despite these changes, undercurrents of unity and conformity are still at work challenging proposals for dramatic structural change. The majority of power positions are still held by members of the dominant culture, but more efforts are made to recruit and hire members from subordinate cultures. People of color hold some positions of power, but generally the higher his or her position, the greater the expectation that he or she will express and demonstrate loyalty to the dominant group's multicultural notion of shared common values and an integrationist discourse.

Within the multicultural institution there are many visible adaptations and a variety of efforts to address issues related to cultural difference. Much effort is also made to appear "culturally conscious" and to incorporate obvious material representations of the institution's commitment to diversity. Some new positions and departments are created to address the expanding needs of the newer members and constituents of the institution. People of color are welcomed into the culture of the institution, so long as they are able to function within the prescribed multicultural vision of those who hold power. It is not unusual for "acceptable" people of color to be utilized in efforts to neutralize those who hold strong radical positions of cultural integrity and who openly acknowledge the existence of cultural conflicts between groups. This practice can cause some fragmentation of leadership among subordinate groups. There is greater acceptance of language differences, but some ambivalence still remains as to the viability and effectiveness of multilingual societies.

Oppositional responses to change from mainstream constituents increase as cultural differences produce tension, conflict, and ambiguity within the institutional environment. Those who have lived within a context of privilege and entitlement now express anger and fear of "losing ground." This can result in backlash efforts by conservatives coupled with a growing hostility toward affirmative action[3] and claims of "reverse racism" when actions are carried out in the interest of diversity. Often institutional transformative efforts are fragmented by those who feel the need to appease any opposition voiced by powerful business, government, church, or political groups.

The research perspective of multicultural institutions most often reflects an acceptance of alternative approaches to producing knowledge. Nonetheless, there still is a strong underlying concern about questions of objectivity and professional distance. As a consequence, some researchers express concerns regarding the validity of diversity studies conducted by women or people of color. Although there is a greater willingness to contend with issues of inequity, often the research continues to reflect a perception of culturally diverse student populations as deficient and in need of compensatory programs. Some elements of cultural relativism and determinism are often present in research on diversity issues at multicultural institutions. The persistence of these views results from the failure of researchers to engage the impact of power in the formation of subordinate cultural values and practices. Institutional tensions surface as people of color collide with power structures that, for the most part, are of the dominant culture. As diversity increases, educational researchers also tend to aggregate groups due to limited numbers and then utilize the results to make group generalizations. Such practices inadvertently lead to distortions in research conclusions and flawed recommendations that perpetuate cultural subordination, despite well-intentioned efforts.

The Culturally Democratic Institution

Within the culturally democratic institution culture is viewed as an integral and fundamental component of the collective, as well as crucial to the individual identity of all human beings. Cultural differences among people are understood and accepted as inherent in any environment that is governed by a strong culturally diverse population. Cultural differences are engaged as common and ongoing occurrences, with tolerance for ambiguity, conflict, and uncertainty. The strengths and limitations of all cultural perspectives that exist within the institution and in society at large are accepted.

The culturally democratic ideological foundation of the institution is shaped by the belief that culture and power are linked and must be understood within the context of historical struggles for voice, participation, and self-determination. This foundation is not only understood with respect to abstract ideals but also in relation to community struggles for the improvement of material conditions. The institutional emphasis is placed on creating conditions for social justice and cultural equality through a dialogical view of working values that are continuously defined and redefined by the historical context and social realities in which people function. Instead of a static notion of specific "shared values," what is shared is the willingness to create working values that can inform institutional decision making.

The distribution of power within a culturally democratic institution is defined in terms of maximum possibilities for structural decentralization. There is greater shared influence and control among the members of the institution. In the interest of social justice and equality, the decentralization of institutional power is also connected to a structure of centralized power in which representative views of all groups are engaged. Multiple spheres within the institution are created to provide the opportunity for expression of cultural integrity and diversity, and for cross-cultural dialogue, decision making, and social action to take place. Within the culturally democratic institution positions of power are redefined in politically equitable, representative, and fair terms, as determined by the social context in which the institution functions. Consequently, people of color hold many positions of leadership, particularly where the interests of specific cultural communities are involved.

The extent of institutional change reflects policies that ensure an ongoing and consistent system of equity. There is greater latitude for the open expression and practice of diversity. The rhetoric diminishes due to an internalized acceptance of cultural differences that is reflected in widespread institutional practices. New and more fluid institutional structures can emerge that support the wider participation of the institution's constituents and the communities it serves.

People of color, just like their white counterparts, are perceived as active "owners" of the institutions. Hence, all are actively involved in shaping the institutional culture as equal participants in the process. Diversity among people of color is recognized and understood as part of the human conditions of all groups. Language differences are accepted and efforts are maximized to cultivate and support multilingualism as a positive and commonplace phenomenon. This view supports the establishment of effective multilingual programs and services that support and encourage the academic success of bilingual and immigrant students. Oppositional responses to change are expected to exist on a continuous basis, as ongoing themes of privilege, entitlement, subordination, and domination surface for all groups, depending on the particular contexts and specific decisions and actions being taken during the historical evolution of a particular institution.

Research methods within a culturally democratic institution are expected to produce knowledge that supports the emancipatory intent of the institution. To facilitate the production of such knowledge, interdisciplinary team research approaches that incorporate a historical, political, and culturally contextualized view of knowledge are utilized. The utilization of diverse approaches to the study of institutional diversity can assist institutions to understand the relationships that exist across the spectrum of human experiences, particularly concerning issues related to social injustice.

In addition, a participatory approach that begins and ends with those who are the subjects of study is strongly encouraged. This approach encourages participants to be involved in the planning and development of the study, the collection of data, the final analysis of the information gathered, and the development of a set of recommendations for institutional action. This research methodology conveys a vision of empowerment by returning to the participants what truly belongs to them, namely, their voice and self-determination. Inherent in this approach is not an attempt to learn *about* people, but to come to know *with them* the reality that challenges them. Through this process, research participates in the discovery of those actions that will function to transform institutional conditions that limit and prevent the enactment of a culturally democratic process (Darder, 1992).

Research in the Interest of Cultural Democracy

Research and its function within an institutional environment are closely linked to the values, beliefs, and practices that are held by those in power. How questions of diversity are framed and defined, the questions that are asked or ignored, and the consequences of institutional research on the lives of subordinate groups are all guided by the prevailing political forces at work. Research in the interest of cultural democracy must be shaped and defined by principles supporting social justice.

In contrast to traditional research that reduces human beings to quantifiable objects in order to predict and control behavior, culturally democratic research begins with the view that human beings participate actively in producing meaning and knowledge in their ongoing interactions with the environment. Research cannot be perceived as a neutral and objective function, but instead must be viewed as an active historical, cultural, and political process of knowledge production. Research must function as a tool for appropriating the codes and cultural symbols of institutional power in an effort to transform institutional environments in the interest of cultural democracy.

Culturally democratic research stimulates constituents to reflect critically upon their world, cultural values and practices, and personal histories so that they may better understand themselves and the social relations of power that affect their lives and shape their social participation. Such research must demystify the artificial limits that are imposed by racism, sexism, classism, and homophobia, by fostering acceptance and understanding of different forms of cultural systems that shape and define diverse communities. Research that supports culturally democratic life must reinforce a language of possibility while acknowledging the human experience of despair that can arise when people must contend daily with the impact of social and economic injustice.

Research in the interest of cultural democracy enables participants to recognize and name their own realities and to understand and assert their own voices within the multitude of discourses present in any institutional environment. It is in essence a critical form of research that stimulates creativity, risk taking, doubting, and questioning in the interest of social justice and equality, while affirming and challenging the strengths and limitations of particular social conditions and institutional realities.

In such a process of study, the researcher can never be perceived as neutral. There is a recognition that knowledge production is always informed by the values and interests of all the participants. It is expected that researchers make their values explicit and make consistent efforts to understand how their values shape their work (Gordon, Miller, and Rollock, 1990). In this way, researchers who carry out their work in the interest of cultural democracy can function as social advocates, facilitating a production of knowledge that is committed to the creation of institutional conditions where people find their voices and their rightful places as full and equal participants.

Notes

1. For an in-depth theoretical discussion of the principles that inform a critical view of cultural democracy, see Darder's Culture and Power in the Classroom (1991).
2. The term critical is used here in its direct relationship to a theory of critical social science. This is to say that "critical" encompasses a view of the world that is both historical and dialectical in nature, which openly acknowledges the cultural, economic, and political dimensions inherent in all forms of knowledge production. Most importantly, it is a view of social science that opposes the positivist tradition inherent in most forms of Western, scientific thought. A significant principle of a critical perspective is its commitment to an emancipatory worldview. For an in-depth discussion of this topic, see Fay's Critical Social Science (1987).
3. For an excellent discussion on the oppositional politics surrounding affirmative action and the impact of the myth of meritocracy upon institutional diversification, see Young's Justice and the Politics of Difference (1990).

References

Crossen, P. "Four-Year College and University Environments for Minority Degree Achievement." Review of Higher Education, 1988, 11 (4), 356–382.

Darder, A. Culture and Power in the Classroom. New York: Bergin & Garvey, 1991.

Darder, A. "Problematizing the Notion of Puerto Ricans as 'Underclass': Toward a Decolonizing Study of Poverty." Hispanic Journal of Behavioral Sciences, 1992, 14 (1), 144–156.

Fay, B. Critical Social Science. New York: Cornell University Press, 1987.

Fisher, F. "Critical Evaluation of Public Policy: A Methodological Case Study." In F. Forester (ed.), *Critical Theory and Public Life.* Cambridge, Mass.: MIT Press, 1985.

Foucault, M. *Power/Knowledge: Selected Interviews and Other Writings.* New York: Pantheon Books, 1977.

Gordon, E., Miller, F., and Rollock, D. "Coping with Communicentric Bias in Knowledge Production in the Social Sciences." *Educational Researcher,* 1990, *19* (3), 14–19.

Jaramillo, M. "Institutional Responsibility in the Provision of Educational Experiences to the Hispanic-American Female Student." In T. McKenna and F. I. Ortiz (eds.), *The Broken Web.* Encino, Calif.: Floricant Press, 1988.

Loo, C., and Rolison. G. "Alienation of Ethnic Minority Students at a Predominantly White University." *Journal of Higher Education,* 1986, *57* (1), 59–77.

Sanders, D. "Cultural Conflicts: An Important Factor in the Academic Failures of American Indian Students." *Journal of Multicultural Counseling and Development,* 1987, *15* (2), 81–90.

Slater, P. *A Dream Deferred.* Boston: Beacon Press, 1991.

Smith, D. "The Challenge for Diversity: Implications for Institutional Research." In M. T. Nettles (ed.), *The Effect of Assessment on Minority Student Participation.* New Directions for Institutional Research, no. 65. San Francisco: Jossey-Bass, 1990.

Smith, K. "Notes from the Epistemological Corner: The Role of Projection in the Creation of Social Science." *Journal of Applied Behavioral Science,* 1990, *26,* 119–127.

Smith, P. *Killing the Spirit: Higher Education in America.* New York: Penguin Books, 1990.

Young, I. *Justice and the Politics of Difference.* Princeton, N.J.: Princeton University Press, 1990.

ANTONIA DARDER *is assistant professor of education at the Claremont Graduate School, where she teaches courses in cultural studies, sociolinguistics, social justice, and critical theory.*

This chapter presents information on the use of portfolio assessment as a planning and evaluation approach for institutions of higher education. The portfolio methodology involves clustering seven critical performance indicators to guide campus efforts in working more realistically with issues of cultural pluralism and diversity.

Charting Campus Progress in Promoting Ethnic Diversity and Cultural Pluralism

Henry T. Ingle

A strikingly different cultural and demographical profile is emerging from the K–12 educational pipeline across the nation as we prepare for dramatic changes that will increasingly characterize the faculty and student body of colleges and universities in the twenty-first century. More-workable approaches to both promoting and assessing the impact of this diversity will be required. One promising new planning and evaluation approach is the use of an institutional portfolio assessment methodology, as herein reported, which speaks to a cluster of seven critical performance indicators that should guide campus efforts in working realistically with issues of cultural pluralism and diversity.

Portfolio assessment offers an alternative approach to institutional assessment of educational change. The terms *alternative, authentic, performance-based,* and *outcomes-based* assessment are often used interchangeably to describe these new assessment practices. The uniqueness of the portfolio assessment approach is that it engages people in real-life problem solving, giving them the opportunity to handle phenomena and situational dilemmas commonly found in day-to-day life and to work with authentic, as opposed to contrived or hypothetical, problems. Through the portfolio assessment approach, mastery or attainment of a particular goal or objective is demonstrated in a variety of ways: an exhibition of the performance under review, investigative research activities, pilot projects, demonstrations, written or oral presentations, or documentation of the effort via video and other electronic media recordings (McDonald, Smith, Turner, Finney, and Barton, 1993). Often, these efforts require collaborative work, brainstorming, and focused problem solving drawn from multiple perspectives. These behaviors, when aggregated, give rise to a portfolio of experiences documenting real "bottom-line" progress in reaching a desired goal. These efforts are examples of the assessment alternatives we think of when we use the term *alternative assessment.*

Portfolio assessment is being advanced by K–12 educators working to improve the traditional, conventional paper-and-pencil testing methods widely used to evaluate student knowledge and achievement, to determine the impact of academic programs, and to conduct self-study appraisals for instructional program improvement, organizational change, and the reformulation of educational policy and practice. The portfolio approach offers a more genuine avenue for both program improvement and educational reform.

Through the work of the Institute for Ethnic Diversity at the Western Interstate Commission for Higher Education (WICHE) in Boulder, Colo., the portfolio assessment approach presented here has been linked to the process of building a pluralistic campus community and learning environment. Supported by the Ford Foundation, the WICHE Institute for Ethnic Diversity has developed an institutional change process designed to assist college and university campuses in their planning and design efforts to promote greater tolerance and understanding of ethnic diversity issues. In the process, the institute also promotes expertise in the creation of teaching–learning environments that reflect the nation's changing population demography and the growing need to make better use of the diversity represented in this human resources base.

The portfolio assessment approach is an integral part of a comprehensive strategic planning and institutional change effort that is being advanced by WICHE. It brings together the relevant "stakeholders" from both the academic and the administrative sides of the campus in a problem-solving mode to address the need for change. The change effort includes representatives from the campus community at large who take part in a series of ongoing dialogues and reflection with the institution's various racial/ethnic groups and an array of specialists and consultants from the outside. These individuals constitute a leadership team that first seeks to understand the new frameworks and paradigms for working with diversity, then defines and assesses the existing campus environment, and finally moves to create a "tailor-made" action plan for promoting diversity on the campus.

The portfolio assessment process begins with, and continues to build upon, the range of what have been termed "difficult dialogues" that historically have characterized most conversations about diversity in America. This is particularly true if the intent is to change the collective group performance and working culture or climate of an organization within the context of diversity.

Coupled with the use of a portfolio assessment approach, the WICHE Institute for Ethnic Diversity helps participating campuses focus on the evolving aspects of diversity and multiculturalism. Like other aspects of campus operations, this requires the development of a comprehensive strategic plan for working proactively with an agenda that highlights the diversity needs at each institution. The effort begins by assessing the campus cultural climate to define the particular diversity issues and operating assumptions that affect the institution. Next, steps are taken to determine how these issues might best be addressed. Including diversity issues in the strategic planning process results in the creation of a sense of overall campus priority for diversity and the development of comprehensive, sustained, and systematic policies, programs, and processes that are compatible with a broad-based set of needs on a particular campus. Key components of the WICHE Institute for Ethnic Diversity strategy include:

The commitment and involvement of the top campus leadership

The ongoing participation of key faculty, staff, students, and representatives from both the campus ethnic communities and the larger academic community

The formation of a core team, involving the president and senior administrators, to give direction and stability to the campus effort

An individualized strategic planning phase coupled with a portfolio assessment process that targets specific indicators or targets of opportunity for diversity change on a particular campus

Use of an experienced cadre of external consultants with expertise in creating multicultural campus environments.

Each plan uniquely reflects the geographic character, historical evolution, and philosophical stance of a particular campus, and therefore the campus plan and the program options selected for working with issues of diversity will also vary, as will the perspectives and practices that are advanced. It is precisely this variation in each of the campus diversity plans that gave rise to the development of the portfolio assessment methodology and the set of critical indicators for charting campus progress with a diversity agenda, as outlined in the following pages.

Portfolio Assessment: What Is It?

The portfolio approach to assessment is gaining in popularity among educators and assessment specialists concerned with new methods for tracking individual student achievement. Portfolio assessment also hold possibilities for charting campuswide institutional change efforts and progress. It is an evaluation methodology designed to capture and integrate individual and collaborative group performance in as close to real-life situations as possible, and includes meaningful opportunities for feedback and self-reflection about progress and success. The process is an authentic test of an individual's abilities because the assessment focuses on the types of behavioral and attitudinal outcomes that promote growth and mastery of important lifelong competencies.

According to Ruth Mitchell (1992), the feature that defines an assessment portfolio as a collection of work is the selection mechanism. Based on the purposes of the assessment, the pieces of work or information included in a portfolio are purposefully selected to demonstrate progress toward a particular goal, a stated aim, or a predetermined set of benchmarks. As such, the portfolio functions simultaneously as a teaching–learning tool for individuals shaping the portfolio and as a feedback mechanism to inform them of their progress. The portfolio assessment approach, in short, facilitates what Dennie Palmer Wolff (1992, p. 17) calls "the footprints of your work"—that is, it documents the cognitive and affective shifts, the ups and downs of your efforts.

Of equal importance to the selection mechanism in the portfolio process is the requirement for self-reflection or the interpretation and the giving of meaning to the pieces of information included in the portfolio. The individual must ask himself or herself, what does the information in the portfolio mean to me and what does it say to others who review it? Embedded in the portfolio approach is a component for self-reflection and comparison that is used to chart the trajectory of progress toward the mastery of the specific set of skills or abilities under review. The process itself can be used to promote significant growth and change over time, both in individuals and within institutions.

The portfolio assessment process is based on a set of mutually agreed-upon performance outcomes and behaviors expected of an individual, or a group of individuals, or—in this case—an institution. This agreement is accomplished through the creation of appropriate scoring rubrics for determining the levels of proficiency in performance. The portfolio assessment process is linked to a specific set of behaviors, at various predetermined proficiency levels that are required to achieve the specified goals. This performance process takes place while an individual, or group of individuals, is engaging in tasks that are typical of the real-life setting and conditions under which the performance is expected to occur.

When transferred to the field of education, portfolio assessment becomes a meaningful exercise in which a person, or group of people, documents behavior and collects information (both of a quantitative and a qualitative nature) in a variety of formats (print, audio, video, and computerized), and of both a subjective and an objective nature, to demonstrate specific progress and the achievement of certain goals in relation to agreed-upon standards of proficiency and excellence. Portfolio assessment relies on the collection and analysis of records, documents, discussions, commentary from self and others, research data, recollections and reflections, and actual observable performance of the skill in question by an individual or a group of individuals. This information is collected over a period of time, in a variety of modes, and is periodically reviewed to show the depth, breadth, and development of the accomplishment of the designated goal or objective.

The key elements of the process require: (1) self-reflection about one's performance; (2) some form of continuous self-monitoring and feedback until the desired level of proficiency is achieved; and (3) constant striving to improve the effort through feedback from both internal and external reviewers.

The use of portfolios represents a collaborative approach to assessment that requires the significant stakeholders in the process to interact with each other as they take specific agreed-upon actions, reflect on the level of effort expended, and learn from the quality of the outcomes and actions taken in terms of the goals or objectives being pursued.

Portfolio Assessment Framework: How Does It Fit into Diversity and Pluralism?

The merits of, and benefits to be derived from, the portfolio assessment process, whether applied to individual group, or institutional performance, lie in the required linkages of what is basically a three-stage iterative, concentric, and upward-moving spiral. Stephen Covey (1989) describes this spiral as: (1) a commitment to change; (2) taking appropriate ownership for and actions to direct the change by doing the things that have to be done; and (3), in the process, learning by doing. Within this paradigm for change, the portfolio process, when applied to the area of ethnic diversity and cultural pluralism, has much intrinsic appeal. This appeal is apparent when one thinks of changing the socialized behaviors and mind-set of a community of people and a style of institutional life that is being redefined as the result of changing demographic and socioeconomic characteristics of the society. Furthermore, the portfolio assessment approach, unlike other, more traditional, evaluation and measurement methods, requires institutions and individuals alike to work with both affective and cognitive data to: (1) change their habits; (2) internalize new principles and patterns of behavior; and (3) integrate three essential ingredients into their new being (Covey, 1989). These ingredients include: knowledge (or "what-to-do" and "why-to-do" behaviors and attitudes); skills ("how-to-do" behaviors); and desire (commitment or "want-to-do" behaviors).

The portfolio process coupled with consultation by outside specialists in the areas of planning for multiculturalism and ethnic diversity offers campus leaders an opportunity to address and evaluate diversity issues. Knowledge developed by the Institute for Ethnic Diversity's intervention process through documentation, analysis, and self-reflection, and the concerns and benefits of diversity ("what-to" and "why-to" behaviors) beget new campus skills ("how-to" behaviors). These skills manifest themselves as outcomes in the form of new, more effective habits.

The portfolio captures "critical incidents" or snapshots of the process as it unfolds on each campus, and allows stakeholders to put a value on them, reflect on the situation, record noticeable progress, and chart the next course of action. This process is pictured in Figure 4.1. In short, it is a real-life performance-based assessment. Furthermore, when all campus portfolios are aggregated over a period of time to look at a common set of diversity goals or objectives, one can reach some larger conclusions about the impact and effects of the diversity change process on college and university campuses. This, then,

Figure 4.1 "Critical Incidents" Portfolio Assessment Process

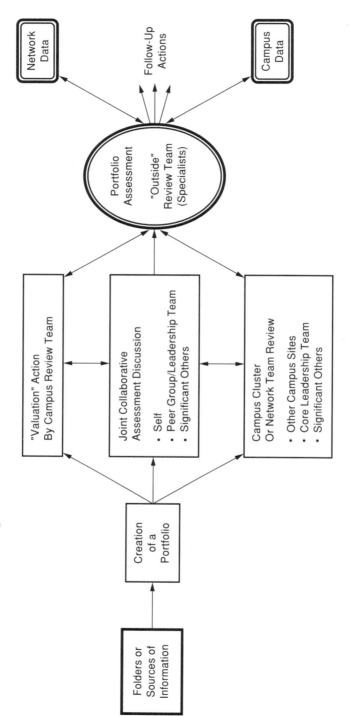

becomes the vision for using the portfolio for assessment on both the individual campus level and across participating campus sites.

Moving from the Individual to the Institutional Assessment Portfolio

This section describes the specific steps needed to implement and pilot-test portfolio assessment on an institutional basis. Particular attention is given to the ways in which portfolios can be used to guide the implementation intervention strategies that have given life to the goals and objectives of the Institute for Ethnic Diversity at WICHE.

The institutional portfolio assessment effort requires an eight-stage process that is initiated with the training of campus representatives. The process requires each campus to set up and track a series of benchmark measures and "critical incidents," policies and practices that can significantly impact the efforts to promote diversity on campus.

A sample listing of these benchmark indicators includes: (1) a campus profile of its student population in terms of the diversity represented; (2) an inventory and description of the conditions for learning success of all students that the campus has in place; (3) a profile of the diversity of the faculty and staff; (4) a genuine appraisal of the quality of campus-community interactions; (5) an assessment of the degree to which there is compatibility between student values and perspectives and the operating norms; mission, and values of the campus; (6) ongoing curricular and instructional revitalization efforts that speak to the concern of educating for diversity; and (7) campus procedures that are in place for communicating about and handling diversity-related conflicts. These benchmark indicators are signposts along the road to promoting diversity that form part of a record to chart progress toward a pre-established level of change in campus performance. Through the portfolio, campus progress is monitored, documented, reflected upon, and evaluated over a period of time by WICHE and the campus stakeholders (faculty, administration, staff, students, trustees, and the community).

The eight stages involved in the development of the institutional portfolio assessment process are as follows:

Stage 1: Past history and performance statement. The campus team develops a comprehensive statement detailing its institution's past performance and history in promoting campus diversity. Trained by WICHE staff and consultants concerning the process of self-reflection and how to conduct focus discussion groups, campus representatives meet a group to develop this history statement. The group candidly engages in self-reflection as it notes areas of success, areas in need of improvement, what has worked, what has not, and the reasons why. This statement of the group's self-reflection becomes the first piece of information placed in the assessment portfolio.

Stage 2: Specification of benchmarks, critical incidents, and key priority indicators. Jointly with WICHE Institute for Ethnic Diversity staff and outside consultants, the institutional history statement is reviewed with campus leaders to identify and create a set of benchmark measures, critical incidents, or key priority indicators, similar to the seven areas earlier identified. They represent the most pressing areas requiring campus attention in terms of diversity and pluralism. The campus will develop a strategic plan to address these concerns as part of its agenda for promoting an institutional climate supportive of ethnic diversity and cultural pluralism. These key indicators give rise to the goals and objectives, along with specified actions and activities that the campus will pursue as part of the portfolio assessment process.

Stage 3: Development of competency levels and scoring rubrics to assess campus performance and progress in specified areas of diversity. In collaboration with the WICHE evaluation team, campus leaders develop the standards of performance that will be used to evaluate the outcomes of the campus efforts. Scoring rubrics are developed to chart the institution's progress along a specified continuum of success and to provide feedback for change and corrections to the course of action.

Stage 4: Collection of information. The portfolio assessment team collects and documents relevant information to monitor and support progress (or lack thereof) on the specified critical performance indicators.

Stage 5: Selection of information. The team selects information to put in a portfolio in support of campus efforts.

Stage 6: Reviewing portfolio. At specified times in the process the Campus Team and WICHE undertake a review and evaluation of items in the portfolio using the pre-established scoring rubrics or performance criteria. They engage in the process of placing value (positive, negative, or "not sure") on the information in the portfolio.

Stage 7: Developing meaning. The Campus Team and WICHE engage in self-reflection and give meaning to the portfolio information. This results in suggestions for change and improvement in the course of action being followed.

Stage 8: Integration. The Campus Team and WICHE staff aggregate and integrate information from their portfolio review process to detect emerging patterns and to pinpoint future actions. Once this activity is completed, the process (Stages 1 through 8) is repeated using outcome measures developed in the prior process.

Institutional progress is monitored and assessed using multifaceted descriptive statements on a scoring sheet or grading matrix, known as a *rubric*. Rubrics are designed to elicit reflection and point the way to increased levels of mastery. Rubrics describe or portray the developmental stages of progression that institutions must master to move further along a predetermined scale of exemplary performance for a given task or set of activities. Rubrics are based upon a mutually agreed-upon set of performance indicators, which are chosen to portray the range of worthwhile tasks or characteristics that need to be operative to demonstrate mastery of a significant task at progressively more demanding and complex levels of performance. As such, rubrics provide assessors with a consistent approach to scoring aspects or elements of both exemplary and nonexemplary performance for a given task or critical performance indicator.

How to standardize the criteria and performance levels used in rubrics at a sufficient level of rigor to support the decisions or judgments being rendered is a key issue for the future development of all authentic assessments. The following eight conditions are normally observed by practitioners developing or devising rubrics: (1) move away from hypothetical situations and look at actual behaviors in real-life situations on campus; (2) do a "loose sort" of the behaviors observed into broad levels of achievement moving from the "least" to the "most" desirable conditions; (3) find strong models or "exemplars" for each scoring point on the scale of least to most desirable; (4) discuss and debate choices of true "exemplars"; (5) identify traits that characterize each level of achievement; (6) record the characteristics into a rubric to keep traits parallel, that is, on a continuum from least to most desirable conditions; (7) start with the perfect response as your top score—if none is located, imagine what the ideal would look like; (8) each descending score on the rubric should describe successively lower levels of achievement or behaviors the campus considers undesirable.

What Goes into the Portfolio?

Just like the use of a portfolio for assessment of an individual's own personal or professional performance, the use of a portfolio assessment approach for institutional assessment can take many forms, including a file or folder of papers, audio and video tapes, photographs, newspaper clippings, letters, memoranda, policy statements, minutes of meetings, written and oral recommendations, campus incidents, anecdotal records, and a variety of graphic and visual products saved on a computer disk. The visuals and charts that follow are illustrative of the variety of items that can be included in a portfolio to document performance and progress.

There are some essential portfolio characteristics that must be observed (Association for Supervision and Curriculum Development, 1992). Portfolio practitioners recommend that:

There must be agreement that informational items and products collected for inclusion in the portfolio illuminate the strengths, weaknesses, areas of improvement, and progress of the organization.

The portfolio must facilitate ongoing assessment by all who are involved in the process. It must serve as a source of self-improvement and change.

For these reasons, the portfolio is not just a collection of the best or most satisfying work, but may also include work that points to unsatisfactory effort. It can suggest risk-taking behavior that can eventually result in successful performance.

Selecting work or informational products to go into the portfolio is a task requiring genuine commitment to the process. The process also requires that portfolio developers and users thoughtfully and critically learn from their efforts in a positive way. The use of the portfolio assessment approach must be tied to the "critical incidents" or priority actions and outcomes that are directly linked to the expected individual or institutional changes being pursued.

Organizing a Portfolio Assessment Approach for Institutional Diversity

Among the biggest challenges facing WICHE's Institute for Ethnic Diversity in using the portfolio approach are the following three concerns. First, we must determine criteria for satisfactory campus performance in the areas of diversity and pluralism. This requires us to ask a question many still have no answer for: "What would a campus that is both espousing and practicing diversity look like?" This question is important to answer at the outset both because of portfolio design considerations and because of the types of changes in performance we expect to see happen. To design an authentic performance-based assessment, such as a portfolio, requires that we first decide what are the actual benchmarks for diversity. This future vision or benchmark we are striving toward needs to come out of the Institute for Ethnic Diversity process.

Benchmarking in this context is the process of evaluating campus operations, policies, and practices to pinpoint weaknesses in the diversity area and then to help identify, study, and imitate or model the behaviors of organizations that excel in those areas (American Society for Training and Development, 1992). By adopting quality standards and practices, campus sites can catapult themselves ahead of their current dilemma and situation, and perhaps even surpass the "benchmarks" to which they aspire. An attempt is made in this section to explore possible answers to this important concern through the presentation of illustrative frameworks and scoring categories. The other two concerns that are in need of attention by WICHE staff and advisers working to implement the Institute for Ethnic Diversity plan include: deciding what goes into the portfolio and determining how best to interpret the contents of a portfolio.

These two latter concerns are perhaps more easily answered than the first. Some assistance in resolving the situation is provided by the writings of diversity specialists Daryl Smith (1990), in *The Challenge of Diversity: Implications for Institutional Research,* and Richardson and Skinner (1991), in *Achieving Quality and Diversity: Universities in a Multicultural Society.* Their observations on the subject also point to some likely responses to the first concern—that is, determining criteria for satisfactory campus performance in the areas of ethnic diversity and cultural pluralism.

Specialists have identified seven conceptual areas of concern that are crucial to both the organizing process and the fundamental transformation of higher education institutions (Smith, 1990). They include:

1. Student body profiles (numerical and qualitative data) that speak to the conditions and resources the campus provides for the success of all students (including special efforts for minority students)
2. Faculty and staff profiles in terms of diversity, that is, numerical and qualitative descriptive data of faculty, administrators, and staff (both permanent and temporary, tenured and nontenured)
3. The quality of the interaction between/among members of the campus community and the academic programs
4. The degree to which there is "synchronization" of student values and perspectives with institutional norms, behaviors, mission, and goals
5. The articulation of a commitment to have educational campus programs work to educate all students about the full range of diversity issues and concerns
6. Campus policies, procedures, and practices for dealing with diversity conflicts on campus (for students, faculty, administrators, and staff)
7. Institutional efforts to clarify perceived conflict between diversity and quality as operating campus assumptions, policies, and practices.

These seven conceptual areas offer some interesting options for creating both a scoring rubric for institutional performance assessment and a continuum along which campuses could rank their progress in promoting a campus climate that incorporates diversity and cultural pluralism. A sample of a companion form to analyze progress on specific institutional diversity goals is included in the Appendix.

Conclusion

Planning and designing a campuswide approach for using portfolio assessment as an institutional evaluation method underscores the fact that it is both an ongoing and lengthy process that requires significant institution-wide commitment and collaboration. There must be consensus on the goals and on the performance tasks to reach these goals and objectives, and on standards and criteria to be used in scoring. Educational practitioners and assessment experts (Association for Supervision and Curriculum Development, 1992) who have been working with issues of pluralism and diversity in the context of the portfolio assessment approach offer the following advice on the creation of these performance-based assessments:

• Pinpoint a diversity goal that is worth achieving. That is, look for tasks that will serve as strong predictors of successful mastery of diversity issues. At the same time, have a rationale for its long-range importance and linkages to the key outcomes expected across the entire instructional program of the campus. Make the assessment task engaging, meaningful, realistic, and challenging so that when the assessment is conducted and the goal is achieved, its significance will be understood and valued. As a result, successful performance of the task will have subsequent ramifications on overall performance in other areas of the campus.

• Establish standards and a scoring system to assess performance that will cause participants to "stretch" beyond their current approaches to problem areas with diversity. The highest score on an assessment of campus efforts should be set beyond the abilities of the best participants so that it can be approached only through commitment, thoughtfulness, persistence, preparation, and significant effort.

• Implement program changes and administer the assessment of their effects on a pilot basis first and have "significant others" review the assessment task and scoring system before its widespread use. This will help ensure that the assessment process is valued, worthwhile, effective, and relevant.

• Once they are refined and pilot-tested, work to institutionalize both the program and assessment approaches so that they become part of everyday practice. This process takes significant time and discussion that can be wearing on the human spirit (Lockwood, 1991). In fact, the biggest obstacle to overcome in the use of the portfolio assessment approach is that of "ensuring" that institution members value the goals and commit to the process. That is, the institution's mission must be different as a result of the assessment or people won't see the need to make the change. There is need for a great deal of collaborative teamwork to successfully adopt and use portfolio assessment approaches.

These cautionary remarks notwithstanding, most educational institutions that have made a commitment to working with portfolios as part of their assessment approach agree that the effort required is worthwhile. The process, they say, gives a major boost to the improvement of the quality of education in most settings, while at the same time enhancing institutional capacity to become more diverse and multicultural in its approaches to teaching and learning.

Appendix

Example 1. Indicators of Campus Progress with Diversity (Holistic Scoring Rubric for Portfolio)

Campus site: _____   Date: _____
Rated by: _____
Title: _____

Directions: For each of the performance categories (A–F) noted below, write in the left margin the performance score level (from levels 1 to 5) that you think

best describes the institution's performance on the basis of your review of the portfolio information provided for each of the performance categories.
Total performance score:

Level 5 = portfolio makes *exceptional case* for diversity
Level 4 = portfolio makes *strong case* for diversity
Level 3 = portfolio makes *adequate case* for diversity
Level 2 = portfolio makes *limited case* for diversity
Level 1 = portfolio *fails to make case* for diversity

Performance Categories: Ethnic Diversity and Cultural Pluralism Indicators

A: Student Profile and Conditions for Learning Success
   Changes in the numbers and percentages of racial and ethnic minorities in the student body:
   Comparison of retention and graduation rates for all students.
   Satisfaction of students with the education experience at campus (students overall and also within specific student groups).
   Performance measures, such as grades, test results, courses taken, and related classroom behavioral measures.
   Feedback from alumni about their campus experiences.
   Programs, activities, and resources the institution provides to promote success for students.
   Special initiatives the institution is pursuing for minority students and the effects of these efforts on their success.
B: Faculty and Staff Diversity Profile
   Demographic makeup and diversity patterns of campus personnel (faculty, administrators and staff, personnel overall and by specific groups and categories) to show changes in numbers and percentages.
   Clustering patterns of minority faculty (special programs, academic department, disciplines and academic fields, tenure and nontenure tracks, and so on).
   Roles minorities are playing on campus in decision making at the student, academic program, and institutional levels.
   Level of satisfaction and longevity among minority faculty and staff (retention).
   Efforts being made for their professional development.
   Degree to which different groups are isolated from mainstream activities of the institution.
   Perceived feelings different campus groups have of being marginalized.
C: Quality of Campus Community Interaction
   Degree to which students of different racial and ethnic groups are involved in the daily life of the institution.

Roles the different kinds of involvement (social, academic, peer, faculty, and so on) play in student performance, persistence, and retention.

Attitudes on campus toward interracial relations and contact.

Feelings students have about campus efforts to value diversity and support cultural pluralism goals.

Support for diversity goals by members of the campus community.

Extent to which campus policies, practices, and the like, are scrutinized and enforced in an effort to promote inclusionary, as opposed to exclusionary, behaviors and attitudes.

Perceptions within campus community about the ways in which negative or intolerable behaviors involving diversity concerns are dealt with.

Description of the general climate on campus in terms of diversity and pluralism.

D: Compatibility of Student Values and Perspective with the Norms, Mission, and Values of Campus Setting

Extent to which the campus institutional way of doing business communicates values that are at odds with the cultures and communities of racial and ethnic minorities.

Extent to which the implicit and explicit values at play on the campus alienate, rather than involve, particular groups.

Ways in which the campus expresses its true feelings and views about goals, values, and beliefs promoting diversity.

Town and gown relationship on campus diversity issues and concerns.

E: Educating for Diversity (Curricular and Instructional Efforts)

Extent to which all students on campus are aware of diversity concerns in their institution, state, and country.

Extent to which students are knowledgeable about and understand ethnic diversity concerns and the histories and cultures of those groups in the society who are different.

Degree to which the curriculum, instructional materials, and media in place on campus reflect new scholarship dealing with issues of race, gender, cultural pluralism, and learning about differences in others.

Degree to which campus as an institution accommodates a range of differences in learning and teaching styles.

Extent to which efforts are made on the campus to involve all faculty and staff in the development and use of new curricular and pedagogical approaches.

F: Campus Procedures for Communicating and Handling Conflict Related to Campus Concerns for Diversity and Pluralism

Level and extent to which conflict about diversity exists on campus.

Ways in which campus as an institution deals with differences and conflict between/among people.

Extent to which differences are valued or viewed as negative.

Degree to which communication on vital issues is satisfactorily handled on the campus.

Extent to which there is an assumption that diversity and quality are at odds.
Measures of performance and success that are in place to minimize problems of bias that may arise on campus.
Types of messages and expectations for success for students, faculty, and staff that are operative in the campus environment.
Types of approaches to policy, planning, and organization for the future that are in place on campus.

Example 2. Sample Institutional Portfolio Assessment and Analysis Form

Campus site: _____ Date: _____
Reviewer: _____
           (name)   (title)

Specific diversity goal objective reviewed:

1. *Performance task(s) under consideration:*

2. *Evidence illustrating campus progress:*

3. *Level at which you would rank campus progress on this task (levels 1 to 5):*

4. *Summary scoring comments and feedback:*

References

American Society for Training and Development. *Understanding Benchmarking: The Search for Best Practices.* Alexandria, Va.: American Society for Training and Development, 1992.
Association for Supervision and Curriculum Development. *Redesigning Assessment: Portfolios.* Washington, D. C.: Association for Supervision and Curriculum Development, 1992.

Covey, S. R. *The Scum Habits of Highly Effective People: Powerful Lessons in Personal Change.* New York: Fireside Books Simon & Schuster, 1989.

Lockwood, A. "From Telling to Coaching for Change: Portfolios." *Focus in Change,* 1991, *1* (3), 3–7.

McDonald, J. P., Smith, S., Turner, D. V., Finney, M., and Barton, E. *Graduation by Exhibition: Assessing Genuine Achievement.* Alexandria, Va.: ASCD Publications, 1993.

Mitchell, R. "Portfolios." In *Testing for Learning: How New Approaches to Evaluation Can Improve American Schools.* New York: Free Press, 1992.

Odell, M., and Mock, J. J. (eds.). *A Crucial Agenda: Making Colleges and Universities Work Better for Minority Students.* Boulder, Colo.: Western Interstate commission for Higher Education, 1989.

Richardson, R. C., and Skinner, E. F. *Achieving Quality and Diversity: Universities in a Multicultural Society.* New York: ACE/Macmillan, 1991.

Smith, D. G. *The Challenge of Diversity: Involvement or Alienation in the Academy.* ASHE-ERIC Higher Education Report, no. 5. Washington, D. C.: ERIC Clearinghouse on Higher Education, School of Education and Human Development, George Washington University.

Smith, D. G. "The Challenge of Diversity: Implications for Institutional Research." In M. T. Nettles (ed.), *The Effect of Assessment on Minority Student Participation.* New Directions for Institutional Research, no. 65. San Francisco: Jossey-Bass, 1990.

HENRY T. INGLE is assistance vice president for technology planning and instructional development at the university of Texas at El Paso, where he is also professor in and chair of the communications department.

This chapter addresses the importance of assessing the campus climate for diversity and the methodological issues associated with this assessment effort.

Assessing Campus Climate: Implications for Diversity

Penny Edgert

Research on student outcomes has consistently concluded that the journey of students through the educational system is correlated with race, ethnicity, and gender (Allen, 1986; Astin, 1992; Pascarella, Smart, and Ethington, 1986; Smith, 1990). That is, knowledge of students' backgrounds allows one to statistically predict, all too well and all too often, the choices that students will make at critical junctions in the educational continuum, the speed at which they will flow through the major transition points, and when and where they will exit the system. For example, the system has been less than successful in preparing African-American, Latino, and Native American students at one educational level for the next one. In addition, this generalization is equally true for Asian and women baccalaureate recipients in terms of advancing to the next educational level (California Postsecondary Education Commission, 1990).

Normally cited as explanations of these differential patterns are factors deemed to be attributable to the student: lack of academic preparation, lack of motivation, dysfunctional family life, lower level of intelligence, or disadvantages resulting from living in a poor community—to name a few. To some extent, these factors may well correlate with variations in academic performance; however, another explanation—certainly more congruent with the issues that surround the quest for greater diversity—is that the educational process *itself* plays a significant role in the different journeys that students of various backgrounds and experiences make through it.

The concept of "campus climate" is gaining currency as one explanation for these differential patterns that are a function of the educational process itself. Thus, better understanding of campus climate may be a critical element in enhancing diversity in our colleges and universities. This chapter attempts to enhance understanding of campus climate in three interrelated ways by discussing: (1) this illusive concept and its importance in making colleges and universities more diverse institutions; (2) assessment strategies that allow institutional decision makers and researchers to explore their own campus climate; and (3) prospective studies that institutional researchers might conduct to examine empirically the relationship between campus climate and quantitative measures of student performance.

Study

Much of the discussion in this chapter emerges from a four-year study of the feasibility of assessing campus climate conducted by the California Postsecondary Education Commission (CPEC), the state agency responsible for long-range planning, policy analysis, and coordination of California higher education. The California governor and legislature directed CPEC to conduct a study to "determine the relative significance of various factors that contribute [sic] or detract from an equitable and high quality educational experience, particularly by women and students from historically underrepresented groups. Of special importance are factors influencing the perceived level of equity being provided in students' educational experiences" (California Postsecondary Education Commission, 1992a, p. 2). The factors of interest in this study were "institutional policies, programs, practices, attitudes and expectations that are conducive to, and serve to encourage the achievement of appropriate educational goals by all students at the institution, in particular women and students from groups traditionally underrepresented in higher education" (California Postsecondary Education Commission, 1992a, p. 2).

Because of the impetus that gave rise to it, this study was broad based and sensitive to the institutional diversity that comprises California higher education. At the same time that this statewide study was being conducted, three California institutions (Stanford, the University of California at Berkeley, and the University of California at Los Angeles [UCLA]) were already engaged in assessing their own climates. These three institutional studies serve to illuminate this discussion with specifics about process and methodological issues.

While much that follows has a California flavor, the demographic shifts in this state—where by the year 2000 no single racial/ethnic group will constitute a majority of the population—makes it a harbinger for the nation. Therefore, California's experiences, particularly in exploring issues related to diversity, ought to be generalizable beyond its own borders.

Concept of Campus Climate

Borrowing a phrase from Bernice Sandler and her colleagues at the Project on the Status and Education of Women (Hall and Sandler, 1982), CPEC defined campus climate as "the formal and informal environment—both institutionally and community-based—in which individuals learn, teach, work and live in a post-secondary setting" (California Postsecondary Education Commission, 1992a, p. 2). As such, campus climate is a collage of the interpersonal and group dynamics that comprise the experience of participants in a collegiate setting.

For the institutional researcher and decision maker the perceptions of individuals participating in a college or university environment provide the lens for viewing campus climate. Moreover, the multiplicity of these perceptions taken together creates a picture of an institution's campus climate as experienced by the people who participate in the college or university community. While this approach may sound extremely relativistic, the fact remains that individuals make decisions on the basis of their perceptions (and seldom on the grounds of objective reality that can be verified and validated by scientific analysis). Therefore, if we seek to understand these decisions and to influence them, it follows that knowledge of individual and collective perceptions is a key to that understanding and influence.

Institutional Self-Assessment of Campus Climate

The CPEC study on campus climate asserted that "[b]y definition, assessment is an introspective, exposing, and vulnerable act, whether of an individual or an institution. While this vulnerability may be axiomatic in general, it is especially true when the topic of assessment goes to the core of institutional receptivity, inclusiveness, and effectiveness—principles to which academic institutions subscribe and value. To explore the extent to which the programs, policies, practices, and attitudes of a college or university support these principles through its actions, then, is a vulnerable and often politically charged risk" (California Postsecondary Education Commission, 1992a, p. 11). This risk may be particularly high with respect to issues of diversity.

Benefits of Institutional Self-Assessment of Campus Climate

Despite, and because of, this very sensitivity, enormous benefits can accrue to an institution from a well-conceptualized and designed assessment of its campus climate:

1. Better understanding of campus climate and its influence on the achievement of diversity goals ought to enhance the capacity and skills of all institutional members to participate in the increasingly multicultural, complex world in which we live.

2. Campus climate influences student performance and the decisions that students make about their educational and career options. As such, information about campus climate may enhance institutional effectiveness and effi-

ciency in terms of student flow measures such as retention and graduation rates.

3. An assessment of campus climate provides a mechanism for shifting discussion from idiosyncratic instances to collective appraisals of institutional life. Campus experiences can be identified in such a way that institutional decision makers can differentiate between singular, isolated, and transitory perceptions and interactions—possibly requiring individual attention—and frequent consistent perceptions that may be rooted in the fabric of the institution.

4. Assessments of campus climate can target institutional strengths and weaknesses so that decision makers can determine which institutional programs, policies, and practices are enhancing the perceived achievement of diversity goals, and establish priorities for actions that the institution should initiate, or continue, to meet those goals.

5. The development of a longitudinal, cyclical assessment system can provide information on the effectiveness of specific, planned interventions designed to achieve diversity goals as well as to identify unplanned institutional changes that may affect the attainment of those goals.

6. Assessing campus climate on a regular basis can allow administrators to act before a major and embarrassing crisis occurs on campus.

Risks Associated with Institutional Self-Assessment

Clearly, risks are associated with institutional self-assessment of campus climate. Undoubtedly, an assessment will reveal for the first time, or confirm, existing perceptions that certain aspects of an institution's climate detract from the achievement of its educational goals, including that of diversity. Depending on the nature and severity of the risks, that identification can create or intensify divisiveness on the campus. While not seeking to minimize the real institutional risks involved, I must point out that the capacity of the institution to create "psychological ownership" among its many constituencies about the assessment can defuse the potential divisiveness that can result, particularly if the assessment is seen as a formative and ongoing rather than as a summative and conclusive process. The development of this ownership should be premised on the knowledge that most, if not all, institutions are less intellectually and socially diverse than they might wish to be, and that discomfort is a natural part of the change process rather than an emotion to fear. Moreover, the assessment can identify the specific ways in which the campus needs to change in order to reach its diversity goals—a critical step in making progress. Lastly, the assessment will identify positive aspects of the environment that heretofore were obscured from view and upon which the institution can be justifiably proud and build.

Because of the sensitivities involved in institutional self-assessment of campus climate, no one formula or cookbook recipe exists. Rather, each campus should determine a process and methodological approach that is most appropriate to its context, mission, goals, and institutional prerogatives.

Importance and Benefits of the Assessment Process

In many ways, the institutional processes developed to conduct the assessment may be as significant to the campus as the results. There are several reasons for this phenomenon. First, the process can create a sense of psychological ownership among constituents because those involved will have a stake in the end product. Second, the assessment process focuses energy and thought on the campus community's own climate—a part of the educational enterprise that seldom holds the attention of institutional constituencies for long, unless a campus crisis exists. Third, profound individual and collective insights often emerge from the assessment process. For example, one faculty member who participated in a field test of the CPEC surveys reported that he began to think about the composition of his classes in different ways than he had previously. Consequently, he examined his records to ascertain if his assignment of course grades was gender-related—an action that resulted in greater knowledge about his own behaviors as they related to gender issues. The assessment process affords the unique opportunity to gain both personal and institutional self-knowledge beneficial to the campus in numerous ways.

Illustrations of Assessment Processes

The Stanford, Berkeley, and UCLA studies of campus climate provide illustrations of the various processes that institutions developed that were consistent with their unique contexts. In this context, process refers to the manner by which the assessment will be conducted, including the impetus for the study, the organizational arrangements for its conduct, the types and levels of institutional participation, and the strategy for monitoring the implementation of study recommendations. A part of the process is the selection of a research methodology—a topic that will be discussed in the next section of this chapter.

Stanford University. Stanford's president and provost established the University Committee on Minority Issues (UCMI) in 1987 for four reasons: (1) to address the rise of intolerance on the nation's college campuses; (2) to create a university community that valued diversity and was "interactively pluralistic"; (3) to respond to a series of racially related incidents at Stanford; and (4) to address the demand of the Rainbow Agenda—a coalition of students from all racial and ethnic backgrounds—that the Stanford community explore their concerns with respect to racism, intolerance, and harassment.

Administratively situated in the Provost's Office, and composed of faculty, students, staff, and individuals from outside the university community, UCMI was directed to set priorities for studying the myriad issues surrounding diversity on the campus; to highlight issues; to identify university policies and practices that might need to be changed; to consult with relevant and appropriate institutional bodies; and to make recommendations to the president.

The report contained a series of far-reaching recommendations (Stanford University, 1989), including the establishment of at least eighteen more regular departmental course offerings to focus on the history and experiences of African-American, Asian American, Latino, and Native American people in this country; the development of resources to assist faculty to incorporate multicultural perspectives in their courses; the creation of a university distribution requirement for the study of Americans from historically underrepresented backgrounds; and the expansion of the Division of Student Affairs's philosophy to include an emphasis on group and community identity in student life.

Following the report's distribution to the campus community and after much discussion, consensus emerged about most of the report's recommendations. The president then established the University Committee on the Status of Multiracial Affairs which, in concert with appropriate institutional offices, committees, and the Stanford Academic Senate, has been responsible for implementing the recommendations and monitoring the movement of the Stanford community toward greater interactive pluralism.

University of California at Berkeley. During the 1980s the University of California at Berkeley made such significant strides with respect to its diversity goals that no single racial or ethnic group constituted a majority of the student body. Despite these gains, the chancellor decided to examine critically the ways in which the institution needed to change in order to accommodate the more diverse student clientele because the campus was approaching a point of real crisis in terms of intolerance, resentment, and lack of community.

The chancellor sought the assistance of a research institution on campus in conducting an exploration of "how the highly variable make-up of students at Berkeley affected their educational and social experience." As such, the study was designed to listen to students to discover the ways in which their education had been influenced by the diversity on campus.

The report presented a series of short-term and long-reaching policy implications and recommendations to the chancellor (University of California at Berkeley, 1990). Four major recommendations emerged from the Diversity Project, specifying that the university should: (1) establish an institutional arrangement whereby in the first six months of his or her time on campus, the student participates in a small group meeting every two or three weeks to address problems of orientation, adjustment, and the integration into campus life; (2) provide institutional support for both "ethnic support groups" and groups that wish to form across racial and ethnic boundaries for a common purpose; (3) widely publicize and give to each student and faculty member information that summarizes admissions policy and affirmative action policy as related to admissions, and that also discusses the relationship between diversity and admissions practices; and (4) identify and encourage a greater role for faculty in stimulating interaction around the curriculum between students from various backgrounds. These implications and recommendations have been, and will continue to be, discussed widely in the university community as it seeks to respond positively to the diversity of the campus.

University of California at Los Angeles (UCLA). In the fall of 1989, UCLA's chancellor requested that the Council on Diversity—an established campus advisory board including broad representation of undergraduate and graduate students, administrators, faculty, and staff—conduct a study focusing campus attention on issues of multiculturalism and community. The council selected a research institute affiliated with the campus to direct the study.

Because of the university administration's desire to generate a sense of involvement and ownership of the study among all campus participants, three task forces were established, each representing one of the major constituent groups of the university: students, faculty, and staff. Throughout the study these task forces provided assistance to the research institute by identifying individuals to participate in the study, assisting in the design of the study, and interpreting the results.

The unpublished report has generated much discussion at UCLA (Astin, Trevino, Wingard, 1991). Once this report is published, the major recommendations about which there is consensus are expected to be implemented on campus, including the core recommendation that the Council on Diversity "strive to develop a comprehensive campus-wide strategy for implementing the proposals for change that have generated such a strong consensus among students, faculty, and staff." Among those proposals are the development of activities to increase interaction and communication among different racial and ethnic groups and between UCLA administrators and students from historically underrepresented backgrounds to introduce more educational activities that focus on diversity.

These three examples illustrate different processes that institutions have adopted to assess their campus climates. Berkeley and UCLA took advantage of the expertise of affiliated research institutes; Stanford and UCLA examined campus climate from the perspective of various institutional constituencies, while Berkeley focused on student voices; Stanford and UCLA established a formal advisory structure to guide their studies, while Berkeley relied on the multicultural composition of its research institute's staff. Despite these and other differences in approach, each of these institutions gained valuable information that should guide them in developing high-quality and equitable learning environments.

Choosing a Methodology

Once an institution has decided to study its climate, the next step is to select an approach by which to gather information, that is, a methodological strategy. As with decisions about process, various methodologies can be used for gathering valuable information. No one methodology is likely to yield the richness of information that a campus needs to gain a comprehensive and intensive picture of its campus climate. Choosing a methodological approach involves decisions with respect to resource expenditures, confidentiality issues, logistical concerns, and the nature of the topics to be explored, among other considerations.

Research indicates that campuses tend to choose one or two methodologies for examining their campus climates. Methods include surveys, group discussions, focused dialogues, individual interviews, outside evaluators, consultants, observations, and document analyses. The use of two of these approaches—surveys and focused dialogues—will be examined in further detail.

Surveys. This approach is especially beneficial in gathering information from a cross section of the campus community, either through random sampling of participants or by surveying all institutional participants. Surveys offer the opportunity to construct a global picture of the campus and to examine a wide range of issues. In addition, surveys are advantagous in that they can be designed to protect the anonymity and confidentiality of the respondents—a particular benefit when exploring issues involving heightened sensitivity in which candor may be less than forthcoming unless respondents' identities can be protected. In terms of resources, surveys are a relatively efficient means by which to gather information in that a minimum of expenditure of human resources is required. At the same time, surveys optimize the number of issues on which information can be gathered at one time. Finally, surveys can be analyzed easily and lead to understandable findings that can be clearly communicated throughout the campus community.

The disadvantages of surveys revolve around their superficial and static nature. That is, surveys constrain the extent to which topics or issues can be explored in depth. While beneficial in "taking the temperature" of the campus, surveys provide minimal information upon which to develop a prescription and treatment plan for the institution. Additionally, surveys are static and provide little or no opportunity to delve into the information provided by respondents. Finally, the impersonal nature of surveys may exacerbate the perceptions of respondents that the institution interacts with its participants in a distant manner.

Both Stanford and UCLA chose to include surveys as one of their methodological strategies. Both designed surveys that were administered to a stratified sample of students, faculty, and staff. Each institution examined actions and policies that affected the existing climate for diversity on campus and sought to identify changes that might lead to a more positive climate for diversity on campus and sought to identify changes that might lead to a more positive climate in the future. Specific topics explored were: (1) curriculum, including availability of courses focusing on the total range of racial and ethnic diversity issues within the United States and incorporation within the existing curriculum of diverse perspectives; (2) faculty, including composition, retention, and career development of faculty from diverse backgrounds, and faculty opinion about students and other faculty from across the spectrum of racial and ethnic groups; (3) movement of students by racial or ethnic groups through the institution, including issues of admissions, financial aid, retention, and graduation; (4) student life, including race relations, social interaction, racism, residential life, ethnic student community centers, and feelings of community; and (5) staff, including composition, inclusiveness, institutional racism, marginalization, institutional mobility, and accountability.

At both UCLA and Stanford the survey responses were aggregated on a total campus basis and disaggregated along the major diversity dimensions, such as racial and ethnic background, gender, and, in the case of UCLA, sexual orientation and nature and extent of disability. The UCLA survey assisted the researchers in developing a comprehensive and intricate picture of campus life, and also allowed for an examination of factors contributing to, or detracting from, diversity goals. Moreover, because the analyses were conducted separately for each major racial and ethnic group, the picture that emerged identified common and unique perceptual patterns and behaviors within and between racial and ethnic groups.

Group Discussion. As its name suggests, group discussion involves assembling sets of participants from one or more identifiable campus constituency groups to discuss their experiences at the institution, usually with the assistance of a trained facilitator. The discussion issues may be predetermined, open-ended, or a combination of both. When the discussion is focused around a particular topic or set of issues, the technique is referred to as a "focus group" methodology.

This methodology is particularly valuable for gathering intensive information on a specific set of topics, and for probing the depth and clarity of perceptions about incidents or tensions on campus. Among other advantages, this approach offers the possibility of gathering serendipitous information and exploring topics not only from an individual but also from a group perspective, at one point in time. Moreover, this strategy provides an opportunity to explore perceptual nuances, sensibilities, and sensitivities. The costs associated with holding group discussions are minimal, except for the expense of a trained facilitator and the time value of on-campus resources.

There are several major disadvantages associated with the group discussion approach. Serious consideration should be given to issues of confidentiality and anonymity—both of which are difficult to protect with this strategy. Moreover, only a limited number of participants can be included in a group discussion and the number of topics that can be covered is likewise circumscribed. In this regard, decisions need to be made about the process for selecting focus group participants and whether that selection is done on a random, a stratified, or a volunteer basis. Finally, only limited types of analyses can be performed on the responses since the information is primarily qualitative and is often impressionistic in nature.

The student-centered Berkeley study selected group discussion as its sole methodology. Two major categories of group arrangements constituted the research design, with many groups in each category. One kind of group was racially or ethnically homogenous, and consisted of four or five students and a facilitator from the same racial or ethnic group. The topics discussed included prior expectations and early entry into student life, study and friendship patterns, social affiliations, experiences of and attitudes toward the concept of racism (especially with respect to the use of admissions policy to further campus diversity), and ways to improve the campus climate, particularly with respect to diversity. A second kind of group was racially or ethnically heterogeneous, and consisted of seven or eight students, with a facilitator selected at random from the institute's research team. The topics discussed included the way in which students "experience ethnic, racial, and cultural exchange," the saliency of diversity in the everyday life of students, and the relevance of racism to the experience of students. By design, the analyses in this study were qualitative, with the research team seeking commonalities and differences in the attitudes and behaviors among and between students characterized along racial and ethnic dimensions.

In the UCLA study, approximately eight focus group meetings were held with students who shared similar backgrounds and campus affiliations, such as membership in fraternities or sororities, political organizations, and so on. The purpose of the focus groups was to identify salient issues around which to construct the survey for campuswide distribution.

Stanford did not choose to use the group discussion methodology in its study. However, Stanford did contract with a consultant to conduct personal interviews with students—a variation on this information-gathering strategy.

As was clear with respect to decisions about process, these institutions selected different methodologies or combinations of methodological approaches. Stanford and UCLA chose multiple approaches, while Berkeley relied exclusively on group discussions. These decisions reflected the differences in the purpose of their assessments. UCLA chose to conduct focus group discussions as well, but for the specific purpose of identifying salient aspects of its campus climate to be included in a survey distributed campuswide. The essential point I wish to make here is that campuses should select methodological approaches that are appropriate to their situation and the purpose of their assessments.

California Postsecondary Education Commission (CPEC) Resource Guide. To facilitate the selection of methodological approaches, CPEC has developed a Resource Guide that seeks to reduce the need to "reinvent the wheel" with respect to institutional self-assessment of campus climate (California Postsecondary Education Commission, 1992b). This guide summarizes more than fifty institutional research studies to which others can refer to learn of methodologies that have been used at other campuses. A second section of the guide contains three pools of survey items—one each for students, faculty, and staff—that institutions can use in any combination or permutation to solicit information from institutional participants. While not meant to be definitive, these item pools can assist campuses to reduce the resources needed for institutional self-assessment of campus climate.

Please refer to Chapter Seven in this volume, on resources, for information on how to obtain both the CPEC Resource Guide and copies of the Berkeley, Stanford, and UCLA reports on campus climate.

Institutional Research Studies on Campus Climate

Beyond gathering and understanding the perceptions of individuals at an institution, institutional researchers might explore other fruitful avenues with respect to campus climate:

1. Of particular significance is the relationship between perceptions of campus climate and student behavior, especially as that behavior is reflected in quantitative measures of performance, such as retention and graduation rates. Correlational analyses could be conducted on an institutional level that relate behavioral measures—grade point averages, time to degree, graduation rates—with campus climate measures. Separate analyses could be undertaken for students based upon their race, ethnicity, or gender.

2. A longitudinal research design could yield information on the association between students' perceptions of campus climate and the decisions they make about their future. Moreover, students could be monitored over time to examine their decisions about pursuing postbaccalaureate studies, choosing careers as faculty members, and the like.

3. In conjunction with other institutions in a local area, on a regional basis, or through a statewide body, case studies could be conducted across colleges and universities to determine the effectiveness of institutional adaptations when such adaptations were suggested by previous assessments of campus climates. A longitudinal design could be developed that monitors, through the use of a survey instrument, the change in perceptions over time of specific institutional adaptations. In this way, it may be possible to gather information of a generalizable nature to assist institutions in enhancing the learning of all students, especially those from backgrounds historically underrepresented in our colleges and universities. While this approach extends beyond the specific institutional setting, its collaborative nature and potential for yielding information valuable to the participating institutions and others may be especially appealing to institutional researchers, particularly if they can, together, obtain support from external funding agencies.

Conclusion

Institutional self-assessment and research is a process predicated on a culture of evidence. The systematic gathering of information on the perceptions of participants provides invaluable evidence—up-close and personal—to institutional decision makers about the nature and quality of campus life. As such, institutional self-studies and planning processes can enrich these examinations, particularly as they relate to diversity. For example, the willingness of a campus to examine the extent to which perceptions of the institution are related, if at all, to the perceiver's racial or ethnic background or gender can indicate whether a specific policy or practice is universally or differentially beneficial or detrimental to the individual or the institution. Depending upon the results of that type of exploration, a series of different actions might be appropriate. However, without that information, campus administrators will be functioning in a vacuum, or "shooting in the dark"—a strategy likely to be both ineffective and inefficient.

The inescapable fact is that an institution will face the challenge of diversity now or face it in the future. Every campus will face the challenge at some point. Understanding the significance of campus climate and understanding one's own campus climate through its systematic assessment is a critical step in meeting that challenge.

References

Allen, W. *Gender and Campus Race Differences in Black Student Academic Performance, Racial Attitudes and College Satisfaction.* Atlanta, Ga.: Southern Education Foundation, 1986.

Astin, A. W. *What Matters in College? Four Critical Years Revisited.* San Francisco: Jossey-Bass, 1992.

Astin, A. W., Trevino, J. G., and Wingard, T. L. *The UCLA Campus Climate for Diversity: Findings from a Campuswide Survey Conducted for the Chancellor's Council on Diversity.* Los Angeles: University of California at Los Angeles, March 1991.

California Postsecondary Education Commission. *Toward an Understanding of Campus Climate: A Report to the Legislature in Response to Assembly Bill 4071.* (Chapter 690, Statutes of 1988). Commission Report 90-19. Sacramento: California Postsecondary Education Commission, June 1990.

California Postsecondary Education Commission. *Assessing Campus Climate: Feasibility of Developing an Educational Equity Assessment System.* Commission Report 92-2. Sacramento: California Postsecondary Education Commission, Jan. 1992a.

California Postsecondary Education Commission. *Resource Guide for Assessing Campus Climate.* Commission Report 92-24. Sacramento: California Postsecondary Education Commission, Aug. 1992b.

California State University. *Campus Climate: Toward Appreciating Diversity.* Long Beach: California State University, Oct. 1990.

Hall, R. M., and Sandler, B. *The Classroom Climate: A Chilly One for Women?* Washington, D.C.: Association of American Colleges, Feb. 1982.

Knutson, K. L. *Differential Treatment: A Prospectus for Legislative Action.* Sacramento: University of California Student Association, 1987.

Pascarella, E. T., Smart, J., and Ethington, C. "Long-Term Persistence of Two-Year College Students." *Research in Higher Education,* 1986, 24 (1), 47–71.

Smith, D. G. "The Challenge of Diversity: Implications for Institutional Research." In M. T. Nettles (ed.), *The Effect of Assessment on Minority Student Participation.* New Directions for Institutional Research, no. 65. San Francisco: Jossey-Bass, 1990.

Stanford University. *Building a Multiracial, Multicultural University Community: Final Report of the University Committee on Minority Issues.* Palo Alto, Calif.: Stanford University, Mar. 1989.

University of California at Berkeley. *The Diversity Project: An Interim Report to the Chancellor.* Berkeley: Institute for the Study of Social Change, University of California at Berkeley, June 1990.

PENNY EDGERT is assistant director for policy analysis at the California Postsecondary Education Commission, the state's planning and coordinating agency for higher education.

This chapter attempts to provide practical suggestions about the special methodological issues that institutional researchers must address while studying and improving diversity in higher education.

Methodological Issues in the Study of Diversity in Higher Education

Marsha J. Hirano-Nakanishi

While the methodological issues in the study of diversity may be approached mechanically, such an approach will misdirect the efforts of researchers. Methodological issues must be placed in the national and institutional context related to diversity. This chapter suggests that by placing institutional research in the context of managing institutional quality, designing research and setting priorities for studying diversity will be facilitated.

Despite variation of opinion regarding increasing diversity in American higher education, most people agree that America is and will become an even more colorful and ethnically diverse place. Indeed, if current trends continue, sometime after 2050 the United States will be a "minority-majority" nation, that is, it will become a nation in which no single group will predominate numerically (Bouvier, 1991b). California will become "minority-majority" any day now under liberal scenarios and before 2010 without continuing immigration (Bouvier, 1991a). Texas and New York are projected to become "minority-majority" within the next twenty to twenty-five years (Marshall and Bouvier, 1985; Bouvier and Briggs, 1988).

The corollary to acceptance of the reality of diversity was enunciated almost ten years ago by David Saxon, departing president of the University of California: "[I]ntelligent self-interest, the welfare of the nation, and justice all demand that we do something" to make sure that the diverse young people of California are educated effectively (quoted in Hodgkinson, 1986, p. 6).

What is meant by *diversity* in higher education and what should be done to achieve it are by no means obvious. Arthur Levine (1991) notes that "bringing more underrepresented populations to campus" was the driving concept of diversity. Representation, which began as an issue focused on students, now

New Directions for Institutional Research, no. 81, Spring 1994   © Jossey-Bass Publishers

embraces staff, faculty, senior administrators, and trustees. Originally *representation* meant an increase from none to a few; today, representation means setting targets in proportion to societal populations. Originally, representation meant access for blacks; today it refers to access for any underrepresented group. "Sustaining the new students who came to campus" was, according to Levine (1991, pp. 4–5), a driving-force concept of the 1970s. Campuses began to provide special scaffolding and stepping-stones—for example, compensatory education, counseling across cultures, ethnic studies programs, and ethnically oriented residential housing—to support students new to and unfamiliar with American higher education. Levine (1991) observes that in reaction to the perceived separatism that evolved from support mechanisms, the agenda of the 1980s was to integrate diversity. New populations were invited to special orientation sessions to facilitate their becoming a part of the campus community; residential houses encouraged integrative support.

In the 1990s acknowledgment of diversity suggests the need for American higher education to re-examine and reshape itself. Diversity in higher education today has evolved into the idea of creating a shared community that maintains the integrity of difference. At one level, this shared community includes orientation programs for all students, providing an introduction not only to the ins-and-outs of university life, but also to the challenges and opportunities of diversity in the community. More fundamentally, the concept of diversity in the 1990s asks faculty to examine whether the curricula are sufficiently diverse and the pedagogy sufficiently developed to inform and prepare *all* students for an interdependent world and an increasingly diverse America.

Levine (1991) notes that definitions of diversity have changed before institutions could complete any of the agendas: representation, support, integration, or multiculturalism. He remarks, "The result today is a jumble of definitions and an assortment of incomplete agendas—a prescription for turmoil" (1991, p. 5). In an ideal world we would clarify definitions, develop a comprehensive action research plan concerning diversity in higher education and, with the time remaining, go about implementing the plan so that children and young people in our diverse cities, states, and country are educated effectively. The institutional research office inevitably finds itself in the middle of these multiple transitions.

Rethinking Higher Education

There is not enough time for decades of research to inform "just" actions. Diversity in higher education will be explosive if left unaddressed. Apartheid in California, driven by unequal education, looms in the future if we fail. Understandably, turmoil and uncertainty characterize higher educational stances on issues of diversity. Levine's (1991, p. 5) urgent call for "presidential leadership, frank and open campuswide discussion, and full involvement of the campus community" in developing plans of action is likely to occur at only a handful of the thousands of university and college campuses at the level and intensity required. Institutions find it difficult to invest scarce time and resources on such volatile and agonizing issues at any time and especially now when the fundamental instruction, research, and public services of colleges and universities are being challenged.

The public and their elected leaders at every level of government are increasingly unwilling to supply all the resources that higher education says it needs and are no longer willing simply to trust the word of higher education that it is doing its job (Korb, 1992; Levine, 1990; Langfitt, 1990; Pew Higher Education Research Program, 1991; Special Study Panel on Education Indicators, 1991; Zemsky and Massy, 1990). If the requirements of diversity in higher education are to be addressed in time to make a difference, they must be interwoven with the more fundamental efforts to rebuild the confidence and support of society.

Consensus appears to be developing that the single-most-important strategy in this rebuilding effort is for colleges and universities to re-emphasize that they are service enterprises in the business of education, that is, teaching students. The Pew Higher Education Research Program (1991, p. 4A) recognizes "just how unsettling the concept may be on first reading. Traditionally, faculty have resisted the notion that they are responsible for their students' learning. . . . We believe, nonetheless, that discussion can benefit from the lessons of other enterprises, both private firms and public agencies, that see themselves as service providers. These lessons are three-fold: (1) know the customer; (2) commit the organization to specific service goals; and (3) establish strong feedback loops that continuously measure the providers' success in achieving these goals."

If national forces compel higher education to emphasize knowing learners better and improving services to them, this focus can coincide nicely with the central call of *One-Third of the Nation* (Commission on Minority Participation, 1988), various advisories on minorities in higher education (within the California State University, see, for example, Arciniega, 1985; California State University Asian Pacific American Education Advisory Committee, 1990; California State University Educational Equity Advisory Council, 1986), and researchers who have focused attention on diversity in higher education (see, for example, Smith, 1990). The extent to which higher education analyzes (gets to know) segmented (including ethnic and language-minority) markets and the extent to which higher education continuously tries ways of effectively reaching and serving increasingly diverse clientele are key indicators of whether higher education is really serving or only paying lip service to diverse learners.

Higher education revenues have not kept pace with expenditures in higher education and are not expected to anytime in the near future (*American Education at a Glance,* 1992). At one time or another, fads from the business world—management by objectives, program-planning budget systems, and zero-based budgeting—have emerged and faded as approaches for effective and efficient administration of higher education. The latest concept, Total Quality Management, known more simply as TQM (Deming, 1986), has been embraced by colleges and universities around the country.

Carothers notes, "TQM is spreading so rapidly and being so well received, not just because it increases efficiency and productivity in difficult times but also because it incorporates a philosophy about work, people and relationships built around humane values and shared vision" (1992, p. 7). TQM increases efficiency, productivity, and sense of community in the enterprise by concentrating on the processes that create products and services by involving stakeholders (Miselis, Lozier, and Teeter, 1992). The key indicator of whether TQM in higher education will come to address issues of diversity is in each institution's mission statement. If educating increasingly diverse Americans for a globally interdependent world is central to the mission of most of America's institutions of higher education, there is continuing hope that we have time to act to address diversity justly and in our self-interest.

While it clearly is too early to tell whether higher education will re-examine and reshape itself around learners, it is equally clear that some part of the change that must take place in higher education to recapture confidence and support must focus on improving services to students. Likewise TQM or CQI—Continuous Quality Improvement (Marchese, 1992a)—teams of frontline faculty and student support staff ultimately may leave little imprint on the way business is done in higher education. Indeed, CQI teams or other versions of dramatically restructured ways of "doing business" may never get formed at many institutions. But President Clinton's and international business leaders' embracings of TQM, CQI, and other redesigns are likely to encourage university communities to try these new approaches, if only to indicate to American political and business leaders that higher education's ivory towers are not hopelessly sealed off from changes in today's world.

Rethinking the Study and Improvement of Diversity in Higher Education

Whether student-centered, continuous quality improvement teams actually serve to reshape higher education, or whether we view them as simply a better way to manage the education enterprise, they appear to be the most viable vehicles by which diversity in higher education can be addressed. There are two major opportunities to interweave diversity into these contemporary vehicles for change: (1) involving diversity researchers in continuous quality improvement processes, and (2) integrating diversity into rebuilding information systems to support monitoring and improving quality.

Involving Diversity Researchers in Continuous Quality Improvement. The most-cited researchers on diversity in higher education also wear the hats of instructional faculty, department chairs, and administrators at various times in their careers and can contribute much to institutional improvement processes, especially in the area of diversity. Integrating their knowledge of diversity into the fabric of institutional improvement processes may not add much to their listings of research publications or help in garnering additional sponsored research support. But it is in an institution's intelligent self-interest to encourage the likes of Walter Allen (see, for example, Allen, 1988), Alexander Astin (see, for example, Astin, 1982; Astin, Trevino, and Wingard, 1991), Richard Duran (see, for example, Duran, 1986), Chalsa Loo (see, for example, Loo and Rolison, 1986), Michael Olivas (see, for example, Olivas, 1986), D. Sanders (see, for example, Sanders, 1987), Daryl Smith (see, for example, Smith, 1990), and Linda Wing (see, for example, Tsang and Wing, 1985), as well as countless disciplinary faculty researchers, like Carlos Cortes (see, for example, Cortes, 1991), Troy Duster (see, for example, Institute for the Study of Student Change, 1990), and Renato Rosaldo (see, for example, Rosaldo, 1992) to join institutional teams charged to make continuous quality improvements to serve their institution's increasingly diverse student body. Whether in universities with a core of researchers and research assistants, liberal arts colleges with interested faculty and upper-division students, or community colleges with involved faculty and staff, there are probably people who should, could, and would help their institution improve services to diverse students, if campus leaders ask for and reward such assistance.

In some instances, a campus's faculty researchers and student research assistants may help to empower frontline staff and teaching colleagues with both useful knowledge about diverse students *and* analytic tools for developing, implementing, and evaluating improvement processes. In addition to the statistical tools associated with TQM (Brassard, 1989), there are powerful qualitative and quantitative methods and tools for gathering and analyzing information about students that are relevant to improving learning and student life. Through the use of focus groups, Duster and his colleagues (Institute for the Study of Student Change, 1990) already have given voice to student suggestions on making the campus more hospitable for people of color and shed light on the ways in which the diverse students at the University of California at Berkeley study, develop friendships, and bridge gulfs among groups. In a similar fashion, Astin and his colleagues at the Higher Education Research Institute (Astin, Trevino, and Wingard, 1991) surveyed students, faculty, and staff at the University of California at Los Angeles (UCLA) to solicit ideas about specific proposals to enhance the climate for diversity.

In other instances, faculty with research interests in diversity may be encouraged to be improvement team members. For example, Harvard University's Assessment Seminars (Light, 1990, 1992) functioned as CQI teams. Harvard now stands at the national center stage for the practical lessons and improvement strategies they have been uncovering and sharing about teaching, learning, and student life simply by asking and answering two basic questions (Marchese, 1992b): "What information can we gather so that we can be more effective teachers and help students to be more effective students next week, next month, next year? How can we all do our jobs better?" Conferences on teaching and learning across the nation have spotlighted Harvard's "discovery" of informal study groups, observations on their role and powerful effects, and suggestions for faculty in improving learning through groups. One wonders at the lessons and strategies that seminars might uncover and share if the participants included more faculty who could contribute relevant projects on diversity to the enterprise.

A hint at the direction in which the seminars might evolve is suggested by anthropologist Renato Rosaldo and his colleagues at Stanford, who survived former U.S. secretary of education Bennett's criticisms of their diversifying introductory courses on culture and civilization at Stanford in 1988. Curricular diversification is not only essential in our rapidly changing world, it is useful for encouraging students to learn and strengthen skills in learning others' perspectives and critical thinking. However, when the professor's own theoretical constructs no longer guide and limit classroom dialogue, teaching and learning are by definition affected. Rosaldo reports that, throughout an advanced seminar in anthropology, he worried at the emotional and discordant dialogue of the seminar discussion among students. He questioned whether he was doing enough, the right things, to ensure that students were thinking more critically and not merely spouting rhetoric; he was surprised and relieved that his most discordant seminar generated the very best of papers—thoughtful, clear and well-defended with evidence (1992). The second report of the Harvard Assessment Seminars (Light, 1992) points out that the single academic goal about which students care most is improving their writing. Diversified curricula may prove to be a most powerful tool for improving critical capacities and effective writing, while also challenging professors' "traditional" notions of good pedagogy.

Rebuilding Information Systems to Support Monitoring and Improving Diversity and Quality. Campus institutional researchers, depending on the organization of the institution, may play similar roles to research faculty in improvement processes. But the fundamental requirement of a campus's institutional research arm is to help the institution to rebuild information systems to support the work of the Continuous Quality Improvement teams and the institutional monitoring of key indicators. TQM and other improvement processes are highly dependent on data analysis to develop, implement, and evaluate plans (Brassard, 1989). Data analysis is by definition decentralized to the team. Even at the University of Pennsylvania, a campus at the TQM vanguard, the university's information architecture is "basically organized around the old way of doing things. . . . [T]o restructure around the actual flow of work, our need is to rebuild information systems so they support the monitoring and improving of quality" (Marna Whittington, quoted in Marchese, 1992c, p. 5).

While current technology permits "user-friendly" data access and analysis capabilities, rebuilt systems will require the consultative and coordinating talents of a central institutional research arm to ensure that teams are getting consistent, valid, and reliable information. In addition, to rebuild confidence and support for the institution externally, regular readings on key indicators of quality are essential, if only to communicate the long-term seriousness with which the institution is addressing consumers' concerns with quality. As trends are established, annual indicator readings and more comprehensive analyses eventually could be characterized as annual checkups and comprehensive examinations on the health of the institution. A central institutional research unit is likely to be the key to coordinating this effort.

The balance of this chapter focuses attention on the two sets of methodological issues that institutional researchers must address to support study and improvement of diversity in higher education within the context of their role in rebuilding institutional information systems.

Diversity in Campus Information Systems: Building the Foundation to Study, Monitor, and Improve

The simplest rule-of-thumb in any collection of data from students is to be as comprehensive and sensitive as possible in asking for information that may prove useful in improving services. In a campus information system, development and maintenance of a few key items on student characteristics (beyond the name, address, identification number) are essential. Date of birth, sex, and race/ethnicity are the three student characteristics that form the foundation of most campus information systems. In addition, at some institutions students have been queried about disabilities or physical challenges to identify and better serve those students who may benefit from specialized services. Other institutions query students on their parents' education to better serve first-generation college-goers.

Birthdate, gender, disabilities, and parental education are relatively easy pieces of information to collect, store, and make accessible. Race/ethnicity, however, is a psycho-socio-political concept. It is fluid and subject to change within an individual. The definitions can change with changing societal norms; and because it is used for the purpose of allocating scarce goods and services, a decision to self-identify or not can have political and economic consequences. Currently, colleges and universities report racial and ethnic information about domestic students (all but nonresident alien students) to the federal government in five broad categories: white, black, Hispanic, Asian/Pacific Islander, and American Indian (Alsalam, Ogle, Thompson, and Smith, 1992), but our most senior institutional researchers can still remember the days when information on race and ethnicity wasn't even requested, let alone reported.

Changing Classifications of Race and Ethnic Origin

In many ways the U.S. census questionnaire provides the best national barometer on the changing conceptualization of race and ethnicity in America.

Earlier in this century, the census provided enumeration only for Caucasoid, Mongoloid, and Negroid. However, because the census is, by definition, a political tool, that is, the data are used to allocate political power, to allocate program funds for the present, and to plan for the future (U.S. Bureau of the Census, 1990a), the census questionnaire changes to reflect a sensitivity to important shareholders in America.

The 1990 "short form" contained seven population and seven housing questions asked of everyone (U.S. Bureau of the Census, 1990b). The Bureau of the Census's use of two of its seven population items to capture information on race/ethnicity reflects the sociopolitical importance of diversity in America. In the first item, "Race," respondents were asked to select whether they are:

- ☐ White
- ☐ Black or Negro
- ☐ Indian (Amer.)
- ☐ Eskimo
- ☐ Aleut

Asian or Pacific Islander (API)

☐ Chinese	☐ Japanese
☐ Filipino	☐ Asian Indian
☐ Hawaiian	☐ Samoan
☐ Korean	☐ Guamanian
☐ Vietnamese	☐ Other API (for example, Hmong, Fijian,Laotian, Thai, Tongan, Pakistani, Cambodian, and so on)

In the second item, "Is this person of Spanish/Hispanic origin?" the choices were:

- ☐ No (not Spanish/Hispanic)
- ☐ Yes, Mexican, Mexican-Am., Chicano
- ☐ Yes, Puerto Rican
- ☐ Yes, Cuban
- ☐ Yes, other Spanish/Hispanic (for example, Argentinean, Colombian, Dominican, Nicaraguan, Salvadorean, Spaniard, and so on)

Blank space was provided with both items to allow respondents to write in, as necessary, the name of a specific, enrolled or principal tribe (for American Indians), a specific Other Asian Pacific Islander race, or a specific Other Spanish/Hispanic origin group.

What began as classifications in physical anthropology have turned into a melange of choices involving race, national origin, and cultural origin. This mix is troublesome to those who do not know nor understand that the census's racial and ethnic classifications are constructed for the purpose of allocating scarce resources. Many wish for tidier classifications and some even hope that scientists, perhaps geographers or physiologists, will somehow come up with a few, unambiguous, fact-based definitions. The battle over the format of the 1990 short-form options, however, may serve to illustrate concretely the sociopolitical reality of race and ethnicity in America.

The 1990 version of the census race and Hispanic-origin items roughly parallels those of the 1980 version. The Bureau of the Census had planned to classify Asians and Pacific Islanders in only one category, "Asian/Pacific Islander," in the 1990 short form instead of the nine provided for in 1980 (Andersen, 1988; Chen, 1987; Lyons, 1987). But Asian and Pacific American communities protested and the California delegation in Washington applied political pressure on the Bureau of the Census. Ultimately the 1980 format for Asian and Pacific Islanders was retained in the 1990 version, and *half* of the twenty racial and ethnic classification bubbles in the census questionnaire ended up as choices for Asians and Pacific Islanders.

The 1990 census-format battle has its roots in earlier decades when it was postulated that aggregated data about Asian Pacific Americans masked the circumstances of disadvantaged subgroups. The 1980 census format finally permitted disaggregated analysis. In the Bureau of the Census's own publication, *We, the Asian and Pacific Islander Americans* (U.S. Bureau of the Census, 1988a), and elsewhere, one indeed found that aggregated 1980 data about Asian Pacific Americans present rosy snapshots about socioeconomic and educational circumstances that mask the dire socioeconomic conditions for Pacific Islanders and Southeast Asians. The percentages of Cambodian, Hmong, and Laotian families living at the poverty level were found to be many times greater than the U.S. average (Hsia and Hirano-Nakanishi, 1989). Because federal service program funds are supposed to be allocated to groups in need and because a primary purpose of the census is to be a tool in this allocation, it ironically is rational and in the service of its mission for the census's racial and ethnic classifications to be unstable and untidy.

In taking the longer view on rebuilding institutional information systems for the future, it is plausible that in the foreseeable future the National Center for Education Statistics and the Bureau of Labor Statistics will ask colleges and universities to provide racial and ethnic data on students and other members of the higher education community in census short-form categories. Already in California, effective January 1, 1990, the state Government Code has been amended to require higher education and other governmental agencies to collect racial and ethnic data to reflect the U.S. census questionnaire's Asian Pacific categories. In addition, state legislative proposals have called for the addition of Thai among Asian Pacifics and Puerto Rican and Cuban among Latinos (Kerschner and Smart, 1990).

Advances in hardware and software technology ought to make it easier and increasingly less expensive for institutions to accommodate changing requirements. Offering students, for example, touch-tone and other on-line opportunities to update information about themselves periodically or whenever they wish should not pose any real technical barriers. Currently, however, for many admissions and records offices, institutional research offices, and computer centers, the entry, maintenance, and reporting capacities of existing information systems form barriers that severely limit institutional capacity to respond swiftly to changing requirements.

Assuming that an institution has the technology and the know-how to accommodate changing definitions of diversity in its information system, it may be worth asking whether one should plan to devise a comprehensive listing of diversity classifications. Again, the existing census questionnaire provides useful context. There were twenty-six population questions and nineteen housing questions asked on the 1990 long or sample form, the additional survey sent out to a 17 percent sample of U.S. households (U.S. Bureau of the Census, 1988b). One open-ended item—"What is [your] ancestry or ethnic origin?"—that was included on both the 1980 and 1990 forms generated thousands of unique responses from which some fascinating findings have come to light (see, for example, James Allen's and Eugene Turner's 1987 award-winning publication, *We the People: An Atlas of America's Ethnic Diversity*).

The census is administered only once every ten years, and enumeration by ancestry has been worth the cost of transcribing and coding handwritten responses once with every census's "blue moon." However, unless significantly more powerful means are developed for electronically handling open-ended responses in operational information systems, the costs for a comprehensive delineation of ancestry and ethnicity are prohibitive. If a campus defines its diversity goal in terms of creating shared community that respects the integrity of difference, it may be worth the cost to the campus to follow the census's "long form" lead on this issue by considering a one-time or decennial survey, a series of focus groups, and a number of one-on-one interviews with members of the campus community to explore diversity in its most comprehensive and broadest senses.

Through such an intensive approach, a campus in the Los Angeles area, for example, could investigate the richness of experience that comes with growing up in the "crazy incubator of Los Angeles" where young people from all colors and cultures "punch holes in stereotypes" and "create a bold, new mix" (George, 1993). Within this context, there are thousands of young college students, like Aileen Cho (1993), who having grown up in multicultural neighborhoods in Los Angeles, are surprised and disappointed to find higher educators holding negative stereotypes that place them light years behind high school teachers. California also has become fertile ground for multiracial marriages and children whose dual identities post personal challenges in seeking community and opportunities for traversing cultural boundaries (Amerasian League, 1990). Continuous Quality Improvement in higher education could benefit from monitoring and learning from these emerging new slants on diversity.

Beyond Indicators of Race and Ethnicity

If it does not make sense to develop a comprehensive listing of racial/ethnic classifications in a campus information system, it may make sense to consider adding some indicators. Color, of course, is the dominant and most powerful factor in educational, social, and economic relations among diverse Americans. Along with Rodney King's and Reginald Denny's beatings in Los Angeles, the killing of Vincent Chin in Detroit because he looked Japanese to some white autoworkers is a dramatic reminder of the progress that we Americans need to make. There is a broad literature on the relationship of diversity factors beyond what people see or think they see—race/ethnicity—to educational and economic achievement (see, for example, Fernandez and Hirano-Nakanishi,1984; S. Garcia, 1980; P. Garcia, 1983; Hakuta, 1986; Hirano-Nakanishi, 1985; Hirano-Nakanishi, Tsang, and Saka, 1991; Hsia, 1988; Hsia and Hirano-Nakanishi, 1989; Lopez, 1976, 1982; McManus, Gould, and Welch, 1983; Nakanishi, 1988, 1989; National Commission on Employment Policy, 1982; Olivas, 1986; Pedraza-Bailey and Sullivan, 1979; Steinberg, Blinde, and Chan, 1984; Sue and Abe, 1988; Suzuki, 1977, 1988; Tienda, 1983; Tsang and Wing, 1985).

If one were to add a few items to an institutional information system on diversity, one might begin by adding an item to tap information about the student and the student's family tenure in this country. Just as knowledge that a student is a first-generation college-goer can help us in orienting the student to the campus, knowledge that a student is an immigrant or refugee (first-generation American) or the son or daughter of one (second-generation American) can provide important cues about a student's familiarity with "mainstream" American culture. An item regarding country of origin, linked to first- and second-generation students, can provide additional, more specific, and relatively unambiguous information about newcomers to the campus who also are new to the United States. Finally, asking all students "How many years have you lived in the United States?," in conjunction with birthdate and date of college entry, can yield information about newcomers' "age on arrival" and "length of stay" in America, providing even more specific and relatively unambiguous additional clues regarding the "cultural baggage" that newcomers carry with them. The more refined our information about a newcomer student's dual-language development and proficiencies and extent of familiarity with American customs and traditions, the better we may help him or her to find community on our college campuses.

With this set of additional information, a campus could monitor and learn more about the Latino and Asian American students who comprise the fastest growing segments of America and American higher education growth in the last two decades (Carter and Wilson, 1992). An institution would be better prepared to monitor, acknowledge, and serve any unanticipated increases in immigrants and refugees from Africa, the Middle East, Eastern Europe, and regions of the former Soviet Union. These people share common challenges and opportunities with Asian and Latino Americans who have entered the educational community in the recent past. Most new arrivals will require intensive ESL instruction and the development of academic English literacy. Many may bring with them a much needed resource in America: fluency and literacy in other world languages. Most would benefit from assistance in acclimating to America and American higher education.

Reaggregating Disaggregated Data

While faculty and staff who are trying to understand and serve their students better may benefit from broad profiles, effective reporting on diversity frequently benefits from uncluttered and specific ethnic comparisons to a white benchmark. Generally, it is difficult to present more than a handful of group statistics in tabular form, and most graphic presentations become cluttered with more than a few series. In analyzing and presenting findings, a good rule-of-thumb is to use both disaggregated and aggregated analyses and to present findings as effectively as possible, while also noting in the discussion and footnotes the extent to which subgroups of larger groups vary.

Until recently, one of the biggest problems faced in research on diversity was the inability to disaggregate data about ethnic and language groups. The major methodological issues now concern the sensitivity required in reaggregation for reporting purposes. The example of the National Educational Longitudinal Study (1988) provides perspective on this. The battle over the format of the 1990 census "short form" was barely over when preliminary results from the National Education Longitudinal Study of the 1988 Eighth Grade Class, more simply known as NELS:88, were released during the 1990 annual meeting of the American Educational Research Association (AERA, 1990). For survey researchers concerned about the education of Asian, Pacific, and Latino language populations, NELS:88, with its supplemental sampling of language minority students and its longitudinal design, promised a rich data source with extraordinary power to inform policy and practices in education from middle school through high school and beyond. Because Latino and Asian American researchers consulted together on issues of sampling, survey items, and implementation in the field, hopes were high in the language minority community.

One major problem with NELS:88 for Asian Pacific researchers was the definition used to create the Asian/Pacific Islander classification. For the Asian/Pacific Islander community that had just prevailed in retaining ten subgroup categories to define Asian and Pacific Islanders in the U.S. Census, it was stupefying to discover that some other wing in the federal government had somehow managed to include Iranians, Afghanis, Turks, Iraqis, Israelis, and Lebanese under the umbrella of Asians and Pacific Islanders. To say that Asian Pacific researchers were dismayed and displeased with preliminary findings is an understatement. Concerns were raised orally at the AERA session on national data sources and minority research, in minority research newsletters, at other national conferences, and in correspondence with Department of Education officials (Hirano-Nakanishi, Tsang, and Saka, 1991).

Similarly, in its first round of reports, *A Profile of the American Eighth Grader* (Hafner, Ingels, Schneider, Stevenson, and Owings, 1990), *Eighth Graders' Reports of Courses Taken During the 1988 Academic Year by Selected Student Characteristics* (Rasinski and West, 1990), and *A Profile of American Eighth-Grade Mathematics and Science Instruction* (Horn, Hafner, and Owings, 1992), there are no technical notes that detail the ethnic subgroups that constituted reporting on Asian and Pacific Islander students. Since over 10 percent of the sample of Asian Pacific students and 15 percent of the weighted sample include students of Middle Eastern, West Asian, and Other Asian descent (Bradby, Owings, and Quinn, 1992), findings about Asian and Pacific Islanders in first-round studies may be problematic.

There is a promising endnote to this continuing saga. In the first follow-up data releases to NELS:88, the technical data file users' manual will detail coding options to permit aggregation consistent with the classification schemes of the Office of Management and Budget (OMB), the Bureau of the Census when it reports on race, and the National Center for Educational Statistics's own Schools and Staffing Survey. Instructions will be provided to assist researchers on grouping only Chinese, Filipino, Japanese, Korean, Southeast Asians (Vietnamese, Laotian, Cambodian, Kampuchean, Thai, and the like), South Asians (Asian Indian, Pakistani, Bangladeshi, Sri Lankan, and so on), and Pacific Islanders (Samoans, Hawaiians, Guamanians, and the like) in the Asian Pacific classification (Ingels, 1992). NELS:88 is an example of an important government commitment to enhance knowledge about ethnic and language minorities.

Issues with aggregation are likely to arise again and again as sociopolitical circumstances shift. As general advice to institutional researchers, the census "short form" provides a good reading on the subgroups and groupings that current national sociopolitical forces have brought to bear. To the extent that this framework is consistent with OMB standards, researchers should feel relatively confident about aggregation algorithms. Sensitivity to regional and local traditions in reporting, however, may prove important to effective communication. It makes sense to constitute formally or informally a group of diverse research and community-based colleagues who can serve as a sounding board on the creation of disaggregated alternatives, reaggregation classification schemes, and naming conventions. Diversity is a fluid concept, and no one person can stay abreast of the most sensitive and useful ways of identifying, grouping, and naming those identities.

Key Indicators: Building the Reading to Track Improvement

Indicators are statistics intended to measure the well-being of a system. The most common indicator system is the annual check up and the periodic comprehensive examination we get from our medical providers that are intended to confirm our general well-being, to monitor improvements, and to signal whether there are particular concerns that may require further examination, diagnosis, and treatment. Likewise, the development of useful indicators in higher education can help us to monitor the health of the enterprise, while signaling areas that may require new or renewed attention. In Harold Hodgkinson's (1985) seminal *All One System: Demographics of Education—Kindergarten through Graduate School,* along with the changing demography of America, he identifies and discusses three important indicators for education, two of which target higher education: (1) retention to high school graduation; (2) transition from school to college: access to college; and (3) completion of college programs: retention to college graduation.

Access to College: Participation as First-Time First-Year Students. In some national and state reports the percentage of persons aged eighteen to nineteen years who are attending college is sometimes implied as an indicator of the transition from high school to college, when, in fact, it unnecessarily confounds the need to improve high school completion with the need to improve the critical transition from high school graduation to college. The American Council on Education recognizes that high school completion is an important education indicator (Carter and Wilson, 1992). It encourages the Bureau of the Census to improve its data collection to permit monitoring of education patterns for all racial and ethnic groups, pointing out that there are two steps in the process to college, first high school completion and then transition.

While national and statewide indicators on the health of the educational enterprise are crucial for informing broad priorities and policies, individual institutions and systems focus on monitoring the extent to which they are effective in serving their special roles in the enterprise in order to confirm progress in areas where special efforts have been made and to identify new areas that may require further examination and action. In California, for example, the Master Plan for Higher Education assigns outreach and education of the top one-eighth of high school graduates to the University of California system (UC), the top one-third to the California State University system (CSU), and the balance to the California Community Colleges (CCC).

California periodically and comprehensively examines, through extensive high school transcript analysis, the extent to which the University of California's and the California State University's admission criteria are both consistent with these assignments and with progress toward achieving equity (California Postsecondary Education Commission, 1992a). The state also is fortunate that K–12 education has developed and maintains the California Basic Education Data System (CBEDS) which provides annual readings on high school graduates and college-prepared high school graduates by racial/ethnic and gender categories at the unit of the high school. For system offices, these data have permitted annual indicators on the extent to which the CSU provides access to California public high school graduates and college-prepared graduates and the extent to which the goal of equity in access is being approached.

Electronic access to CBEDS data is used by individual campuses of the CSU in the spirit of Continuous Quality Improvement. It is worthwhile to describe the measures that have proven useful. CBEDS data on racial/ethnic and gender enrollments for middle and junior high schools have been used for identifying and planning early outreach programs. Data on tenth and eleventh graders at key feeder high schools have formed the basis for annual outreach plans. These outreach efforts are targeted on increasing the academic pre- paredness of adolescents through early support and encouragement and on improving information sharing and early support in preparation for and com- pletion of college admission and financial aid applications. The joining of CSU campus application flow data (records by high school of applications, admis- sions, and first-time freshman enrollment) and CBEDS high school graduate data have made it possible for campus enrollment managers to monitor the cumulative effectiveness of various outreach efforts aimed at key feeder high schools in encouraging eligible students to prepare, apply, and enroll. Much of the success that CSU campuses and diverse students have enjoyed in match- ing students' readiness and desire to attend college with informative and timely outreach has been supported by the ability of institutions to use campus data sources and external data sources in planning, implementing, and evaluating efforts.

Access to College: The Transfer Function. P. Garcia (1992) notes that although some observers believe that the ties between two-year and four-year colleges and universities have weakened over the years, the larger problem is the absence of adequate definitions and data to quantify transfer activity. In a state like California that has premised its Master Plan for Higher Education on the vitality and validity of the transfer function, these inadequacies loom large. For the California State University, where two-thirds of new undergraduate stu- dents are transfers, these inadequacies undermine monitoring effectiveness in addressing mission.

After several years of deliberations, representatives from each segment of California public higher education have forged an agreement to identify a cohort of California Community College first-time, first-year students who are "potential" transfer students, to collect annual student level data on persistence and transfer, and to calculate statewide transfer rates based on common stan- dards (Intersegmental Coordinating Council, 1992).

As important as these baseline transfer rates to the UC and to the CSU will be, overall and by ethnicity, other indicators on the transfer function are equally important. For the CSU, which has awarded eight of every ten public baccalaureate degrees to students who started at a California community col- lege (California Postsecondary Education Commission, 1992b), the comple- mentary issues of age-at-entry and time-to-transfer are important facets of the transfer function that have implications for the nature and timing of outreach through community colleges. Unpublished data from the CSU suggest that while half of all community college transfers come to the CSU within five years of high school graduation, at nine years after high school graduation the critical mass of transfers has only reached 75 percent. It will make a difference in plans for improving the transfer function if the transfers reflect delayed entry as community college first-time first-year students (that is, they begin college as older students), or if the time-to-transfer is primary.

Retention to College Graduation: Persistence and Time to Degree. In 1985 Hodgkinson stated the issue eloquently: "It seems important to point out that the 'template' for undergraduate education (eight semesters of instruction straight through to graduation) has not been the path taken by even a simple majority of students over the years. Our response has tended to be criticizing part-time and older students with family and job responsibilities rather than revising the template so that the length of a student's education is variable" (p. 17). Recent reports have indicated that even for those institutions whose selectivity and status, residential character, cost to family, and preparedness of incoming students have at least provided settings conducive to high four-year graduation rates (see Pascarella and Terenzini, 1991, for a comprehensive review of the literature), the "four-year bachelor's degree is a thing of the past for the vast majority of students" (National Institute of Independent Colleges and Universities, 1989, p. 4).

From Hodgkinson's basic suggestion, the CSU has recast its template on persistence to graduation. In 1987 the CSU surveyed a sample of graduates who took five years or longer to receive the baccalaureate (Robb, 1988). Because it is in the CSU's mission to serve the nontraditional undergraduate who often is precariously balancing work, school, and family, the survey revealed the "difficulties that many Californians encounter in earning their . . . collegiate degree while engaged in all the responsible tasks of adult life" (California Postsecondary Education Commission, 1988, p. 17). Over 90 percent of the students who took longer than five years to graduate worked while attending school. While one in six student-workers might be characterized as typical work–study students, four in six reported working twenty to thirty-nine hours per week, and the remaining sixth was working forty hours or more. For the vast majority of students who took more than five years to graduate, much more time was spent at work than in the classroom. In addition, about one-quarter of all the respondents took some time off from school—from one to three terms—and another 10 percent took off four terms or more. Again, for students who are juggling responsibilities, economic realities and other personal priorities sometimes take precedence over school and the student must temporarily "stop out." The CSU concluded that, while campuses should continue to seek ways to improve scheduling and advising, lengthened time to degree was, in large measure, reflective of the special circumstances and preferences of CSU students (Robb, 1988). To the extent that the CSU's mission continues to include serving able, but nontraditional, students, it stands by the principle that a student's pacing to degree, by definition, must be variable.

When reframed to extend beyond four-, five-, or even six-year contexts, the news about persistence to degree reveals improved and even dogged persistence to graduation (California State University, 1990). If the five-year persistence rate (that is, the percentage of first-time first-year students who have either graduated or are still enrolled in school at the five-year mark) continues to provide a good indicator of eventual graduation, then the 1983 cohort of CSU first-time freshmen will demonstrate a 20 percent increase in persistence to eventual graduation over its 1973 cohort. This terrific forecast is even more meaningful when understood in the context of an increasingly diverse first-time first-year class and apparently increasing requirements for students to juggle life priorities.

Other Important Indicators and Tools. Many additional indicators and tools need to be developed and employed by institutional researchers to monitor and improve higher education. Annual and periodic surveys of student needs, priorities, and perceptions regarding importance, quality, and costs of a variety of institutional policies, procedures, and programs, for example, provide important readings about student satisfaction and concerns (see California State University, 1989, for a policy report based on three waves of student surveys). Surveys of employers and alumni also provide important external suggestions and readings on the effectiveness of instruction and services. And certainly, the faculty's continuing responsibilities in assessing students' learning and in improving personal pedagogy must continue to be central in the educational enterprise (California State University Institute for Teaching and Learning, 1992). Important discussions must begin to take place on the extent to which campus information systems can be redesigned to assist faculty in monitoring and assessing students' learning.

Surveys and assessments raise some special issues for diverse students, and there are a few lessons to share from the K–12 experience. In NELS:88, appropriate sensitivity was demonstrated in considerations regarding the multiple-choice achievement testing of very-limited-English-proficient students. Limited-English-proficient students appropriately were excused from the ordeal of taking multiple-choice achievement tests written in English. Alternative forms of assessing these eighth graders' knowledge and skills were explored briefly in preliminary planning discussions, but costs were high and funding sources unavailable. Unfortunately, the very limited-English-proficient students also were excused from completing the base-year sample survey altogether, even though personal information and perceptions from these students could have been gathered with relative ease on site. Because some Asian Pacific and Latino subgroups are almost exclusively comprised of recent immigrants, the exclusion of very limited-English-proficient students could have amounted to their complete dismissal from the survey. Generally, it was acknowledged that the educational and socioeconomic profiles of Latino and Asian Pacific eighth graders in NELS:88 may not be sufficiently representative of Latino and Asian Pacific eighth graders nationally given the exclusion of potentially significant portions of those student groups. Fortunately, a commitment was made to refresh the national sample with a survey of excluded students (Hirano-Nakanishi, Tsang, and Saka, 1991; Ingels, 1991).

As an institution considers new directions in understanding and address-ing student needs, the sounding board of diverse research and community-based colleagues, suggested earlier to advise on the creation of disaggregated alternatives, reaggregation classification schemes, and naming conventions with regard to race and ethnicity, also can prove invaluable in survey and assessment methodologies. As a final piece of advice, we institutional researchers must learn to feel comfortable in reaching out and asking questions to do our jobs well generally and especially with regard to diversity. Many facets of life in higher education are changing; conceptually and methodolog-ically we will be challenged to invent and do things that we've never done before. Improvement teams, sounding boards, and other ways of communi-cating and changing are important to our improved effectiveness.

Conclusion

It is in our own enlightened self-interest to effectively incorporate the reality of diversity in higher education. Resources are thin and expected to remain so, and even in the best of times the comprehensive study of diversity in higher education has not placed at the top of research support lists. There is neither the time, the resources, nor the will to study everything we'd like about diver-sity in higher education to guide and improve representation, support, inte-gration, and multiculturalism on campuses.

National forces appear to be encouraging higher education to refocus its attention on improving service to the student. Continuous Quality Improve-ment processes are gaining momentum. While these processes may not emphasize the diversity of the student, unless the increasingly diverse pool of young people are excluded from higher education (which would be fatal for American higher education and society), by definition, addressing issues of diversity in higher education is central to the success of continuous-quality-improvement.

Continuous Quality Improvement teams and institutions will benefit from the inclusion of researchers who are knowledgeable and interested in issues of diversity in higher education. It is also essential that institution information systems be rebuilt to provide CQI teams with ready access to critical informa-tion about diverse students and to provide annual and periodic readings on the progress that the institution is making in improving both quality and diver-sity in higher education.

References

Allen, J. P., and Turner, E. J. *We the People: An Atlas of America's Ethnic Diversity.* New York: Macmillan, 1987.

Allen, W. "Black Students in U.S. Higher Education: Toward Improved Access, Adjustment, and Achievement." *Urban Review,* 1988, *20* (3), 165–188.

Alsalam, N., Ogle, L. T., Thompson R. G., and Smith, T. M. *The Condition of Education 1992.* NCES 92-096. Report of the National Center for Education Statistics, Office of Educational Research and Improvement, U.S. Department of Education. Washington, D.C.: U.S. Government Printing Office, June 1992.

Amerasian League. "Japanese American/American Japanese: On Being Multi-Racial Japanese in Modern Times." In *Multi-Racial Asian Times* (a newsletter of the Amerasian League, Santa Monica, Calif.), 1990, pp. 5–9.

American Education at a Glance. Washington, D.C.: National Center for Education Statistics. (ED 343946)

American Education Research Association (AERA). *1991 AERA Annual Meeting Program.* Washington, D.C.: American Education Research Association, 1990.

Andersen, P. "Critics: Census on Asian Still Unclear." *Asian Week,* Mar. 25, 1988, pp. 1, 24.

Arciniega, T. *Hispanics and Higher Education: A CSU Imperative.* Long Beach: Office of the Chancellor, California State University, 1985.

Astin, A. W. *Minorities in American Higher Education: Recent Trends, Current Prospects, and Recommendations.* San Francisco: Jossey-Bass, 1982.

Astin, A. W., Trevino, J. G., and Wingard, T. L. *The UCLA Campus Climate for Diversity: Findings from a Campus-Wide Survey Conducted for the Chancellor's Council on Diversity.* Los Angeles: University of California at Los Angeles, Mar. 1991.

Bouvier, L. F. *Fifty Million Californians?* Washington, D.C.: Center for Immigration Studies, 1991a.

Bouvier, L. F. *Peaceful Invasions: Immigration and Changing America.* Lanham, Md.: University Press of America, 1991b.

Bouvier, L. F., and Briggs, V. *The Population and Labor Force of New York.* Washington, D.C.: Population Reference Bureau, 1988.

Bradby, D., Owings, J., and Quinn, P. *Language Characteristics and Academic Achievement: A Look at Asian and Hispanic Eighth Graders.* NCES 92-479. Statistical Analysis Report of the National Center for Education Statistics, Office of Educational Research and Improvement, U.S. Department of Education. Washington, D.C.: U.S. Government Printing Office, Feb. 1992.

Brassard, M. *The Memory Jogger Plus+: Featuring the Seven Management and Planning Tools.* Methuen, Mass.: GOAL/QPC, 1989.

California Postsecondary Education Commission. *Time to Degree in California's Public Universities: Factors Contributing to the Length of Time Undergraduates Take to Earn Their Bachelor's Degree.* Commission Report 88-12. Sacramento: California Postsecondary Education Commission, Mar. 1988.

California Postsecondary Education Commission. *Eligibility of California's 1990 High School Graduates for Admission to the State's Public Universities.* Commission Report 92-14. Sacramento: California Postsecondary Education Commission, June 1992a.

California Postsecondary Education Commission. *Student Profiles 1991.* Commission Report 92-10. Sacramento: California Postsecondary Education Commission, Mar. 1992b.

California State University. *A Survey of Student Needs and Priorities 1989.* Long Beach: Academic Affairs, Office of the Chancellor, California State University, 1989.

Those Who Stay: 1983 First-Time Freshmen—Student Persistence in the California State University. Long Beach: Division of Analytic Studies, Office of the Chancellor, California State University, Oct. 1990.

California State University Asian Pacific American Education Advisory Committee. *Enriching California's Future: Asian Pacific Americans in the CSU.* Long Beach: Office of the Chancellor, California State University, 1990.

California State University Educational Equity Advisory Council. *Educational Equity in the California State University: Which Way the Future?* Long Beach: Office of the Chancellor, California State University, 1986.

California State University Institute for Teaching and Learning. *Student Outcome Assessment: What Makes It Work?* Long Beach: Institute for Teaching and Learning, California State University, 1992.

Carothers, R. L. "Trippingly on the Tongue: Translating Quality for the Academy." *AAHE Bulletin,* 1992, *45* (3), 6–10.

Carter, D. J., and Wilson, R. *Minorities in Higher Education: Tenth Annual Status Report.* Washington, D.C.: Office of Minorities in Higher Education, American Council on Education, Jan. 1992.

Chen, S. "Asians Fear Proposed Census Form Will Have a Negative Impact." *East/West News,* Nov. 19, 1987, pp. 1–2.

Cho, A. "A Little Patch of Diversity." *Los Angeles Times,* Feb. 3, 1993, p. B7.

Commission on Minority Participation in Education and American Life. *One-Third of a Nation.* Washington, D.C.: American Council on Education, 1988.

Cortes, C. E. "Pluribus & Unum: The Quest for Community Amid Diversity." *Change,* 1991, 23 (5), 4–5.

Deming, W. E. *Out of the Crisis.* Cambridge: Center for Advanced Engineering Studies, Massachusetts Institute of Technology, 1986.

Duran, R. "Prediction of Hispanics' College Achievement." In M. A. Olivas (ed.), *Latino College Students.* New York: Teachers College Press, 1986.

Fernandez, R. M., and Hirano-Nakanishi, M. J. *Critical Transitions for Hispanic Youth: A Report on High School Dropping Out, Postsecondary School Attendance and Labor Force Experiences, Based on High School and Beyond Base-Year and First Follow-Up Surveys.* Contractor's Report to the National Center for Educational Statistics. Los Alamitos, Calif.: National Center for Bilingual Research, 1984.

Garcia, P. *Dual-Language Characteristics and Earnings: Male Mexican Workers in the United States.* Los Angeles: Population Research Laboratory, University of Southern California, 1983.

Garcia, P. *Projections of Enrollment Demand, 1990 to 2005.* Long Beach: Office of the Chancellor, California State University, Sept. 1991.

Garcia, P. "Operationalizing the Transfer Function." Paper presented at Leadership 2000, the fourth annual Leadership Conference on Leadership Development in Community Colleges, Chicago, July 19–22, 1992.

Garcia, S. *Language Usage and the Status Attainment of Chicano Males.* Center for Demography and Ecology Working Paper no. 80-2. Madison: University of Wisconsin, 1980.

George, L. "Brave New World: Gray Boys, Funky Aztecs and Honorary Homegirls." *Los Angeles Times Magazine,* Jan. 17, 1993, pp. 14–17, 36–38.

Hafner, A., Ingels, S., Schneider, B., Stevenson, D., and Owings, J. A. *A Profile of the American Eighth Grader: NELS:88 Student Descriptive Summary.* NCES 90-458. Statistical Analysis Report, National Center for Education Statistics, Office of Educational Research and Improvement, U.S. Department of Education. Washington, D.C.: U.S. Government Printing Office, June 1990.

Hakuta, K. *Mirror of Language: The Debate on Bilingualism.* Seattle: University of Washington Press, 1986.

Hirano-Nakanishi, M. J. "Academic Achievement Among Asian Americans: Some Old and New Issues." Paper presented at the University of California Conference on Linguistic Minorities, Lake Tahoe, Calif., May 1985.

Hirano-Nakanishi, M. J., Tsang, S., and Saka, T. "The National Education Longitudinal Study of 1988 (NELS:88), Asian Pacifics, and Language Minority Students." Paper present at the annual meeting of the American Education Research Association, Chicago, Apr. 4, 1991.

Hodgkinson, H. L. *All One System: Demographics of Education—Kindergarten through Graduate School.* Washington, D.C.: Institute for Educational Leadership, June 1985.

Hodgkinson, H. L. *California: The State and Its Educational System.* Washington, D.C.: Institute for Educational Leadership, June 1986.

Horn, L., Hafner, A., and Owings, J. *A Profile of American Eighth-Grade Mathematics and Science Instruction.* NCES 92-486. Statistical Analysis Report of the National Center for Education Statistics, Office of Educational Research and Improvement, U.S. Department of Education. Washington, D.C.: U.S. Government Printing Office, June 1992.

Hsia, J. *Asian Americans in Higher Education and at Work.* Hillsdale, N.J.: Erlbaum, 1988.

Hsia, J., and Hirano-Nakanishi, M. "The Demographics of Diversity: Asian Americans and Higher Education," *Change,* 1989, *21,* 20–27.

Ingels, S. "The Problem of Excluded Baseline Students in a School-Based Longitudinal Study: Correcting National Dropout Estimates and Accommodating Eligibility Change over Time." Paper presented at the annual meeting of the American Education Research Association, Chicago, Apr. 6, 1991.

Ingels, S. *National Educational Longitudinal Study of 1988 Base-Year/First Follow-Up: Student Component Data File Users' Manual.* Draft. Chicago: National Opinion Research Center, 1992.

Institute for the Study of Student Change. "The Diversity Project: An Interim Report to the Chancellor." Berkeley: University of California at Berkeley, June 1990.

Intersegmental Coordinating Council. "Assessing the California Transfer Function: The Transfer Rate and Its Measure." Conclusions of the Data Needs Task Force, Sacramento, Calif., Feb. 1992.

Kerschner, L. R., and Smart, J. M. Memorandum to Presidents on Additional Ethnic Code Classifications. Long Beach: California State University, May 9, 1990.

Korb, R. *Postsecondary Student Outcomes: A Feasibility Study.* NCES 92-013. Report of the National Center for Education Statistics, Office of Educational Research and Improvement, U.S. Department of Education. Washington, D.C.: U.S. Government Printing Office, Feb. 1992.

Langfitt, T. W. "The Cost of Higher Education: Lessons to Learn from the Health Care Industry." *Change,* 1990, *22* (6), 8–15.

Levine, A. "Editorial: The Clock Is Ticking." *Change,* 1990, *22* (6), 4–5.

Levine, A. "Editorial: The Meaning of Diversity." *Change,* 1991, *23* (5), 4–5.

Light, R. J. "The Harvard Assessment Seminars: First Report—Explorations with Students and Faculty About Teaching, Learning, and Student Life." Cambridge, Mass.: Graduate School of Education and Kennedy School of Government, Harvard University, 1990.

Light, R. J. "The Harvard Assessment Seminars: Second Report—Explorations with Students and Faculty About Teaching, Learning, and Student Life." Cambridge, Mass.: Graduate School of Education and Kennedy School of Government, Harvard University, 1992.

Loo, C., and Rolison, G. "Alienation of Ethnic Minority Students at a Predominantly White University." *Journal of Higher Education,* 1986, *57,* 58–77.

Lopez. D. E. "The Social Consequences of Chicano Home-School Bilingualism." *Social Problems,* 1976, *24,* 234–246.

Lopez, D. E. "The Effect of Schooling Abroad on the Socioeconomic and Language Patterns of First Generation Hispanics and East Asians." Technical Note 7. Los Alamitos, Calif.: National Center for Bilingual Research, 1982.

Lyons, J. A. "Professors Blast Census Plans for Asians in 1990." *Asian Week,* Dec. 11, 1987, pp. 16–17.

Marchese, T. "AAHE and TQM (. . . Make that 'CQI')," *AAHE Bulletin,* 1992a, *45* (3), 11.

Marchese, T. "Assessing Learning at Harvard: One Institution's Continuing Search for What Works Well, What Doesn't, and What to Do About It—An Interview with Richard J. Light." *AAHE Bulletin,* 1992b, *44* (6), 3.

Marchese, T. "TQM at Penn: A Report on First Experiences—An Interview with Marna C. Whittington." *AAHE Bulletin,* 1992c, *45* (3), 3–5.

Marshall, F. R., and Bouvier, L. F. *The Future Population of Texas.* Washington,D.C.: Population Reference Bureau, 1985.

McManus, W., Gould, W., and Welch, F. "Earnings of Hispanic Men: The Role of English Language Proficiency." *Journal of Labor Economics,* 1983, *1,* 101–130.

Miselis, K. L., Lozier, G. G., and Teeter, D. J. "Strategic Planning and Total Quality Management: A New Partnership." Paper presented at the 32d annual forum of the Association for Institutional Research, Atlanta, May 10–13, 1992.

Nakanishi, D.T. "Asian Pacific Americans and Selective Undergraduate Admissions." *Journal of College Admission,* 1988, *118,* 17–26.

Nakanishi, D. T. "A Quota on Excellence? The Asian American Admissions Debate." *Change,* 1989, *22,* 38–47.

National Commission for Employment Policy. *Hispanics and Jobs: Barriers to Progress.* Report no. 14. Washington, D.C.: National Commission for Employment Policy, 1982.

National Institute of Independent Colleges and Universities. *Undergraduate Completion and Persistence at Four-Year Colleges and Universities.* Washington, D.C.: National Institute of Independent Colleges and Universities, 1989.

Olivas, M. A. (ed.). *Latino College Students.* New York: Teachers College Press, 1986.

Pascarella, E. T., and Terenzini, P. T. *How College Affects Students: Findings and Insights from Twenty Years of Research.* San Francisco: Jossey-Bass, 1991.

Pedraza-Bailey, S., and Sullivan, T. "Bilingual Education in the Reception of Political Immigrants; The Case of Cubans in Miami, Florida." In R. V. Padilla (ed.), *Ethnoperspectives in Bilingual Education Research: Bilingual Education and Public Policy in the United States.* Ypsilanti: Department of Foreign Languages and Bilingual Studies, Eastern Michigan University, 1979.

Pew Higher Education Research Program. "Learning Slope." In *Policy Perspectives,* 1991, 41a. Philadelphia: Institute for Research on Higher Education, University of Pennsylvania.

Rasinski, K. A., and West, J. *Eighth Graders' Reports of Courses Taken During the 1988 Academic Year by Selected Student Characteristics.* NCES 92-479. E.D. Tabs of the National Center for Education Statistics, Office of Educational Research and Improvement, U.S. Department of Education. Washington, D.C.: U.S. Government Printing Office, July 1990.

Robb, P. S. "California State University: Factors Affecting the Time to Degree." Report in Response to the Supplementary Language to the 1987/88 Budget Act. Long Beach: Division of Analytic Studies, Office of the Chancellor, California State University, Jan. 1988.

Rosaldo, R. "Symbolic Violence: The Western Culture Controversy at Stanford." Public lecture read at the University of Wisconsin, Madison, Oct. 6, 1988; the University of Washington, May 5, 1989; Swarthmore College, Feb. 16, 1990; the University of California, Berkeley, Feb. 28, 1990; the University of Richmond, Apr. 11, 1990; and the University of Texas, Austin, Apr. 18, 1990.

Rosaldo, R. "Cultural Citizenship and Educational Democracy." Keynote address given at the Postsecondary Division (J) of the American Education Research Association's annual meeting, San Francisco, Apr. 1992.

Sanders, D. "Cultural Conflicts: An Important Factor in the Academic Failures of American Indian Students." *Journal of Multicultural Counseling and Development,* 1987, *15* (2), 81–90.

Smith, D. G. "The Challenge of Diversity: Implications for Institutional Research." In M. T. Nettles (ed.), *The Effect of Assessment on Minority Student Participation.* New Directions for Institutional Research, no. 65. San Francisco: Jossey-Bass, 1990.

Special Study Panel on Education Indicators. *Education Counts: An Indicator System to Monitor the Nation's Educational Health.* Report to the Acting Commissioner of Education Statistics, Office of Educational Research and Improvement, U.S. Department of Education. Washington, D.C.: U.S. Government Printing Office, Sept. 1991.

Steinberg, L., Blinde, P. L., and Chan, K. S. "Dropping Out Among Language Minority Youth." *Review of Educational Research,* 1984, *54* (1), 113–132.

Sue, S., and Abe, J. *Predictors of Academic Achievement Among Asian American and White Students.* New York: College Entrance Examination Board, 1988.

Suzuki, B. H. "Education and the Socialization of Asian Americans: A Revisionist Analysis of the 'Model Minority' Thesis." *Amerasia Journal,* 1977, *4,* 21–51.

Suzuki, B.H. "Asian Americans in Higher Education: Impact of Changing Demographics and Other Social Forces." Paper presented at a Ford Foundation National Symposium on the Changing Demographics of Higher Education, New York, Apr. 8, 1988.

Tienda, M. "Market Characteristics and Hispanic Earnings: A Comparison of Natives and Immigrants." *Social Problems,* 1983, *31* (1), 59–72.

Tsang, S., and Wing, L. C. "Beyond Angel Island: The Education of Asian Americans." *ERIC/CUE Urban Diversity Series,* 1985, *90,* 45.

U.S. Bureau of the Census. *We, the Asian and Pacific Islander Americans.* Washington, D.C.: U.S. Government Printing Office, 1988a.

U.S. Bureau of the Census. *1980 Census Population: Asian and Pacific Islander Population in the United States.* Washington, D.C.: U.S. Government Printing Office, 1988b.

U.S. Bureau of the Census. *Census '90 Basics.* Washington, D.C.: U.S. Government Printing Office, 1990a.

U.S. Bureau of the Census. *1990 Census Questionnaire.* Washington, D.C.: U.S. Government Printing Office, 1990b.

Zemsky, R., and Massy, W. F. "Cost Containment: Committing to a New Economic Reality." *Change,* 1990, 22 (6), 16–22.

MARSHA J. HIRANO-NAKANISHI is director of the division of analytic studies in the system office of the California State University.

This chapter provides institutional researchers with information
about a variety of resources to help them assess diversity on their
campuses.

Assessing Diversity on Campus:
A Resource Guide

Thomas Levitan, Lisa E. Wolf

Once an institution decides to assess its success in addressing issues of diversity, the institutional researcher is faced with an important question: How? Fortunately, a number of institutions, researchers, and scholars have attempted to answer this question and there is much to learn from previous attempts to address this issue. This compilation of diversity-related resources includes different institutional approaches, a variety of resource clearinghouses, publications, and electronic mail (e-mail) listings germane to institutional research.

The range of approaches to assessing diversity is as varied as institutions of higher education themselves. Some institutions, for example, survey the full spectrum of campus constituents: students, faculty, and staff. Other institutions aim their assessment at only one constituency. Still other institutions target members of diverse groups—"the other"—as a means to understand the institutional climate for diversity, rather than questioning the entire population. Specific institutional techniques include surveys, interviews, focus discussions, and all-campus forums. Even the definition of *diversity* varies from institution to institution, with some institutions choosing to focus on racial and ethnic groups, gender, sexual orientation, or the physically challenged, while other institutions examine the full range of difference. Each institution approaches its research differently, taking into account institutional goals, available resources, size and type of institution, and the researcher's skills.

The annotated list of instruments and books in this chapter is a starting point for the institutional researcher to develop an appropriate methodology for her or his campus. One of the best ways to engage in assessing diversity is to enter into dialogue with others who share the same task. The e-mail lists included in this resource chapter provide a forum for this type of discussion.

NEW DIRECTIONS FOR INSTITUTIONAL RESEARCH, no. 81, Spring 1994   © Jossey-Bass Publishers

The researcher's task in a culturally democratic institution is to engage in the research as an active participant, and to allow constituents to participate in the creation of the methodology and to voice their own perceptions of the institution. This chapter provides the institutional researcher with the tools to engage in such a task.

Institutions That Have Conducted Diversity Assessments

Diversity of the Community Survey
Student Affairs Research and Evaluation Office
Arizona State University
Tempe, Ariz. 85287-3001
Tel: (602) 965-4070
Contact: S. Leellen Brigman

Arizona State has developed a survey that questions whether students take advantage of opportunities to interact with people who are different from themselves. The survey asks, for example, how many people from various groups the respondent has conversed with during the past twelve months and about the respondent's perceptions of different groups of people. By asking students to comment on the extent to which they have observed members of various groups experiencing different types of discrimination, the survey itself heightens students' awareness of racism and discrimination. Copies of the survey are available.

Cultural Diversity Survey (in progress)
Office of Institutional Research
Bowling Green State University
Bowling Green, Ohio 43403-0023
Contact: James L. Litwin

Bowling Green, a comprehensive state university, created a survey to assist in understanding the impact of a newly required general education course on cultural diversity. The goal of the survey is to measure the impact of the course on students, not to determine students' satisfaction with the course. The nine-question survey is administered to students after they have completed the course. It includes questions about what cultural diversity means to the student, student attitudes concerning the required course, what the student thinks she or he has learned, what changes have taken place in the student's attitudes and beliefs about race and ethnicity, and what the student thinks about the "melting pot" of American society. There is also a question about whether students plan to take another diversity course. Copies of the survey are available.

Climate Surveys, 1992
Office of Institutional Advancement
North Seattle Community College
9600 College Way North
Seattle, Wash. 98103-3599
Contact: Scott Kerlin

In 1992 North Seattle Community College surveyed faculty, staff, and students to determine their attitudes and perceptions concerning campus climate. The survey was administered as part of a pretest to help the institution "create a climate where cultural diversity is recognized and valued." The posttest will be administered in five years. Separate surveys were administered to all employees (including all full and part-time faculty, classified and hourly/part-time staff, and administrators) and to a sample of students. Thirty common questions ask respondents about their level of agreement with statements on a variety of topics relating to diversity and climate. These include questions about the individual's own experiences, her or his observations of the experiences of others, and things the institution *ought* to do to improve the climate. Both surveys query respondents about whether their attitudes and views of those who are different have changed as a result of their experiences at the college. The student survey adds ten questions dealing with student experiences in and out of the classroom. The faculty and staff survey asks respondents to indicate how long they plan to remain part of the college community; this question is important given the transient nature of the community college population. Copies of the surveys and compiled responses, as well as a program for presentation of the results, are available.

Enhancing Diversity: Toward a Better Campus Climate. A Report of
    the Committee on Lesbian and Gay Concerns, 1992
Center for the Study of Higher Education
Pennsylvania State University
403 S. Allen, #104
University Park, Pa. 16801-5252
Tel: (814) 865-8367
Contact: Estela Bensimon

The committee on Lesbian and Gay Concerns at Pennsylvania State University surveyed all faculty and staff and a random sample of students to assess prevailing campus attitudes toward lesbians, gays, and bisexuals. The survey ad-dresses the extent to which individuals have contact with gays, lesbians, and bisexuals. It also asks respondents to indicate how likely it is that gay, lesbian, and bisexual campus constituents will experience certain types of discrimination; specifically, these questions address the possibility of harassment, inability to find off-campus housing, and comfort level with being "out of the closet." Questions also address how respondents would feel about working with some-one who is gay, having a gay roommate, having a gay professor, or being alone with someone who is gay. In general, the results of the surveys indicate atti-tudes and beliefs held by the heterosexual population on campus. To address these issues from the viewpoint of homosexuals on campus, the committee chose to interview lesbian and gay faculty and staff. The methodology allowed interviewees who are not "out" to the campus community to participate in interviews while maintaining their confidentiality. These interviews illuminate the daily challenges and indignities faced by these constituents and provide a depth of understanding on the issue from the viewpoint of the targeted popu-lation. Copies of the surveys, and a report of both the precise methodology and the results, are available.

Student Campus Climate Survey, 1991
Office of Planning and Development
Scripps College
Claremont, Calif. 91711
Contact: Brenda Barham-Hill

Scripps College, a small, highly selective women's college, surveyed its returning students to assess their perceptions of the campus climate for diver-sity. With a target population of only 427 students, Scripps administered the instrument to the entire returning student body. The two-page survey gathers limited demographic data about the students. Respondents are also asked to indicate their perceptions about diversity on campus and to indicate whether they have had a roommate of a different background. The survey asks students to indicate their level of agreement with twenty-six statements dealing with diversity. These questions cover issues about the in- and out-of-class environ-ment, the individual's own feelings of acceptance and isolation on campus, and changes that the student has experienced in her own ability to deal with issues of diversity. Three open-ended questions offer the student the opportunity to note major concerns about campus climate at Scripps. Copies of the survey and compiled responses are available.

Final Report of the University Committee on Minority Issues, 1989
Office of Multicultural Development
Building 10
Stanford University
Stanford, Calif. 94305
Tel: (415) 723-3484
Contact: Sharon Parker

Stanford University, as described in both Penny Edgert's and Marsha Naka nishi's chapters in this volume, conducted an assessment of its climate using student surveys and individual interviews. The final report of the results demonstrates how institutions can convert survey findings to significant institutional recommendations. Copies of the final report are available.

The Diversity Project: Final Report
Institute for Social Change
2420 Bowditch
University of California at Berkeley
Berkeley, Calif. 94720
Tel: (415) 642-0813
Contact: Troy Duster, Director

The University of California at Berkeley conducted an institutional climate assessment via the use of focused group discussions. For a description of the methodology, please refer to Penny Edgert's chapter in this volume. Copies of the final report are available.

Student, Faculty and Staff Surveys on Diversity, 1990
Higher Education Research Institute
320 Moore Hall
Graduate School of Education
University of California at Los Angeles
405 Hilgard Avenue
Los Angeles, Calif. 90024-1521
Tel: (310) 825-1925

As mentioned in Penny Edgert's chapter, UCLA conducted an assessment of its institutional climate. While UCLA held focus group meetings, they also depended heavily on the use of multiple-choice survey data. The institutional researchers created three surveys: one for faculty, one for students, and one for staff. All three surveys elicit information about the general climate at UCLA, attitudes about diversity, respondents' experiences at UCLA, and their ratings of the efficacy of possible institutional solutions. Each questionnaire has a slightly different focus to capture the relevant information from each group. For example, the faculty survey elicits information on departmental climate, joint research opportunities, and tenure and promotion policies. The student questionnaire asks about perceptions of the faculty and the presence or absence of role models. Finally, the staff survey elicits information about hiring and promotion issues and about the work environment. Copies of the surveys and of the final report are available.

Perspectives on Campus Diversity: A Survey of C.U. Boulder
   Undergraduates, 1990
Office of Research and Testing
Campus Box 108
University of Colorado at Boulder
Boulder, Colo., 80309
Contact: Lou McLelland

The Office of Research and Testing at the University of Colorado at Boulder developed a survey of student perceptions on diversity. The survey is designed to be administered to all students and addresses a broad range of diversity-related topics, including feelings of acceptance, comfort on the campus, perceptions of how individual students are treated, personal attitudes, and satisfaction with services. The survey also allows respondents to provide narrative responses. One question, for example, asks students who report being verbally harassed for racial or ethnic reasons to describe the incident. Another question asks students to describe incidents in which they have been the subject of racial stereotyping. In addition, students are asked to describe the university from the viewpoint of a minority student. Analysis of the survey is broken down by student demographic characteristics, feelings about campus race issues, and responses to programs and services. Copies of the survey and compiled responses are available.

Report on the Self-Reflective Study and
   All-University Forum on Diversity, 1992
Office of Student Affairs
120 Morrill Hall
University of Minnesota, Twin Cities Campus
100 Church St. SE
Minneapolis, Minn. 55455
Tel: (612) 625-0368
Contact: Nuri Hassamani

The University of Minnesota used a qualitative research method to assess the institution's climate for diversity, making "no pretension about the neutrality of the study." Specifically, the researchers interviewed over ninety faculty, staff, administrators, and students from marginalized groups to attempt to understand their "hopes and dreams," and to determine what further institutional efforts needed to be considered. The interview format was unstructured to elicit responses about the issues that came to mind as people conversed; interviews lasted approximately one hour. Participants were selected from the membership rosters of various task forces and campus committees, through recommendations of others, and through the researchers' knowledge of individuals who have a history of working with issues of diversity and pluralism on campus. The results of the interviews were presented at an all-university forum so that the broader campus community could add their voices to those of the persons interviewed. Copies of the final report—*All-University Forum on Diversity: Attending to Human Details*—are available.

Comprehensive Survey on Diversity
Office of Student Affairs Research
110 Morrill Hall
University of Minnesota, Twin Cities Campus
100 Church St. SE
Minneapolis, Minn. 55455
Tel: (612) 626-0746
Contact: Eric Scouten, Research Projects Coordinator

The University of Minnesota at Twin Cities campus conducted a comprehensive survey of diversity during the spring of 1993. The instrument addresses several dimensions of diversity, including sex, race, sexual orientation, disability, native language, and religious background. Topics addressed include the climate for diversity (for example, harassment, graffiti, insensitive remarks, supporting remarks), students' willingness to interact with those who are members of other groups, specific student services, personal actions relative to diversity, experiences as a member of various subgroups on campus, and what the university can do to improve its climate for diversity. This survey instrument will be mailed to a random sample of undergraduate students from among the various racial and ethnic groups, to disabled students, and to gay/lesbian/bisexual/transgender student groups. The university will share its instruments, as well as a report of the results of the survey.

Student Climate Survey, 1992
124 Administration Building
University of Nebraska at Lincoln
Lincoln, Neb. 68588-0423
Tel: (402) 472-3755
Contact; John Harris, Vice-Chancellor for Student Affairs

The University of Nebraska at Lincoln devised a student opinion survey as a means to assess institutional climate. Nebraska's efforts were limited to an analysis of ethnic and racial diversity issues. Multiple-choice questions cover a number of important dimensions of campus life including interaction with faculty and administration, student services, facilities, and academic involvement. In addition, the survey includes a number of opinion items about the institution's response to racism, inclusion in the classroom, experiences with "the other," experiences with racism, and university policies regarding race. Copies of the survey and compiled responses, as well as a program for presentation of the results, are available.

System-Wide Assessment of Diversity, 1988
The University of Wisconsin System
Madison, Wis. 53706
Tel: (608) 262-8636
Contact: Dr. Andrea-Teresa Arenas,
Acting Special Assistant to the President for Minority Affairs

The University of Wisconsin's program is noteworthy because it represents a systemwide attempt at assessing institutional climate and at maintaining uniform information on the needs of underrepresented students, faculty, and staff. *The Design for Diversity Plan* (1988) represents the system's preliminary steps to address issues of multiculturalism and to outline goals for the improvement of evaluation efforts in the areas of minority student enrollment/retention and faculty/staff recruitment and retention. The assessment protocol of the University of Wisconsin system requires each institution to implement a uniform minority information system as a way of obtaining cross-institutional comparisons. The system office has committed a high-level staff person to oversee the program and to consult with the individual campuses on their efforts. This resource is helpful for those contemplating implementing systemwide evaluation strategies. Copies of the *Design for Diversity* are available.

Diversity Resource Collections

Achieving the Promise in Diversity: A Research Agenda
    to Inform the Issues, 1991
American Association for Higher Education Research Forum
Alverno College
P.O. Box 343922
Milwaukee, Wis. 53234-3922
Tel: (414) 382-6263
Contact: Marcia Mentkowski

Each year prior to the annual American Association for Higher Education (AAHE) meeting, the association has convened a preconference forum concerning the general topic of the meeting. The forum brings together educators and researchers to identify and discuss research that will actually benefit higher education policy and practice. The results are compiled as a list of research questions relevant to the annual topic. The 1991 forum focused on "Achieving the Promise of Diversity." The forum developed a broad list of research questions concerning issues of diversity—"The Professoriate," "Teaching to Student Learning Differences and for Diversity," "Conflict on Campus," "Curricular Debate: Common Culture, Co-curriculum, and Inclusiveness," "Global Diversity/Global Interdependence," and "Toward Diversity in the Research Model." While research questions raised in each category may not be directly related to the on-campus work of the institutional researcher, the different approaches to framing questions can be valuable in developing institutional research activities.

Resource Guide for Assessing Campus Climate
California Postsecondary Education Commission
1303 J Street, Fifth Floor
Sacramento, Calif. 95814-3298

California Postsecondary Education Commission (CPEC), the coordinating board for higher education in California, produced an extraordinary resource guide for assessing diversity issues. The resource guide is divided into two sections. The first offers a review of methods and processes for studying campus climate, including surveys, group discussions, and analysis of institutional documents. The resource guide includes a discussion of the strengths and weaknesses of these various techniques. The second section of the guide includes pools of survey and discussion questions for use with students, faculty, and staff. The questions were developed through a process of focus groups, review, and field testing at public, independent, and community colleges in California. Copies of the guide are available.

Clearinghouse for Higher Education Assessment Instruments
1819 Andy Holt Avenue
Knoxville, Tenn. 37996-4350
Tel: (615) 974-2350
Contact: Jama Bradley, Michael Smith, Gwynetta Draper

The University of Tennessee at Knoxville's clearinghouse for assessment instruments provides annotated lists of survey instruments. Although the collection is comprehensive, many of the instruments are dated. The surveys related to diversity include the University Alienation Scale from the University of Virginia, designed to assess feelings of alienation experienced by African-American students, and the Multicultural Attitude Questionnaire of the College of Education at Virginia Polytechnic and State University. Since many of the surveys available at the Clearinghouse measure attitudes toward people who are "the other," they may be useful in developing instruments to measure the impact of campus activities. Specifically, surveys could be administered prior to the campus activity to determine a baseline and then re-administered to measure change in attitudes.

Project on the Status and Education of Women
Association of American Colleges
1818 R Street, N.W.
Washington, D.C. 20009
Contact: Bernice Sandler

The Project on the Status and Education of Women has developed several surveys and numerous reports that address the experiences of women students, faculty, and staff in American higher education. The majority of the project's work focuses on gender-based discrimination felt by various members of the campus community. One questionnaire asks women faculty members to define sexual harassment, to reflect on gender-based behaviors in the classroom, and to recount the number of times they have experienced various types of sexual behavior from colleagues or authority figures. A student survey elicits women student's responses to inappropriate behavior; their experiences of inappropriate behavior from other students, faculty, and administrators; and their experience of the current campus climate for women students. Similar instruments are available that address gender-based discrimination experienced by women of color from different campus constituents. Copies of surveys and reports are available.

Books and Articles Useful in Assessing Diversity

Green, M. F. *Minorities on Campus: A Handbook on Enhancing Diversity.* Washington, D.C.: American Council on Education, 1989.

This handbook offers the reader a broad range of resources and ideas for assessing diversity. Chapters are devoted to the institutional diversity audit, students, faculty, administration, climate, and teaching and the curriculum. Each chapter begins with an introductory section on the current situation and includes strategies for enhancing diversity, as well as programs and resources for acting on these strategies. Methods of assessing success are also included. The book contains descriptions of successful campus programs in each area.

Keller, G. D., Deneen, J. R., and Magallán, R. J. (Eds.). *Assessment and Access: Hispanics in Higher Education.* Albany: State University of New York Press, 1991.

For remaining doubters concerning the need for new means of assessment for students of color and others, this book should resolve their doubts. The editors have collected the research of test specialists and researchers in the higher education community, as well as data from the Educational Testing Service, in several areas relating to Hispanic students: elements that affect Hispanic performance on standardized tests and therefore admission to higher education and even entry into the teaching profession; elements of test construction as it affects Hispanic students; and the development of *TestSkills*, a pilot kit to be used by teachers of Hispanic high school students to prepare them for college admissions tests. The value of this volume is in making clear and indisputable the cultural values and biases that underlie standardized tests.

Kuh, G. D., Schuh, J. H. Whitt, E. J., and Associates. *Involving Colleges: Successful Approaches to Fostering Student Learning and Development Outside the Classroom.* San Francisco: Jossey-Bass, 1991.

Involving Colleges demonstrates a lens and a methodology not specific to diversity but mirroring the advice and outlook offered in this volume. The institutional audit model, like the portfolio approach, examines a broad range of components of institutional activity. Chapter 11 describes eleven general principles to serve as guidelines for institutional discovery and understanding. Among the principles are the following: culture is both the lens through which institutional participants interpret and make meaning of their world and "the glue that binds an institution"; an institution and its cultures must be examined from the perspectives of its members to create a complex, comprehensive description of the institution; campus audits should not be conducted exclusively by insiders *or* exclusively by outsiders; an institution must use qualitative research methods to understand and discover its culture. In addition to these principles, the authors provide two resource chapters that describe their methodology and provide a protocol for institutions to use in assessing their climate. The protocol focuses on climate issues, with special emphasis on students' out-of-class experiences. The questions direct attention to the multiple factors that may influence student involvement.

Nettles, M. T. (Ed.) *The Effect of Assessment on Minority Student Participation.* New Directions for Institutional Research, no. 65. San Francisco: Jossey-Bass, Spring 1990.

This issue of *New Directions for Institutional Research* focuses on the student aspect of assessing diversity. Specifically, it discusses issues of precollegiate preparation for college, the effects of emerging outcomes-assessment policies on minority student achievement, the organizational and structural changes needed by colleges and universities to improve performance of minority students, and minority student access to graduate schools and careers that have rigorous assessment criteria for entry. Seven articles are included in this issue. Among the articles are "Assessing Program Effectiveness in an Institution with a Diverse Student Body," by Mildred Garcia; "The Effects of Assessment on Minority Participation and Achievement in Higher Education," by Roy McTarnaghan; and "The Challenge of Diversity: Implications for Institutional Research," by Daryl Smith.

Richardson, R. C., Jr., and Skinner, E. F. *Achieving Quality and Diversity: Universities in a Multicultural Society.* New York: American Council on Education-Macmillan, 1991.

The Department of Education's Office of Educational Research and Improvement funded a study of ten predominantly white colleges that have been especially effective in educating American students of color. This volume is a collection of case studies of those ten institutions. Although none of the individual case studies provide models for assessing success in diversity, as a whole the case studies provide the reader with a review of the various components of the environment that might be examined. The volume concludes with recommended actions for institutions to take to achieve diversity and quality. The authors suggest a three-stage model. The first stage involves efforts to improve access by developing recruiting and admissions practices to increase enrollment of typically underrepresented students. The second stage, principally carried out by student affairs staffs, includes the creation of programs and services to support students. In the third stage, the institution fully adapts by recognizing preparation gaps in students, learning outcomes expected by the students, and ways that the institution is not meeting student needs. The learning process is transformed by the institution. The techniques used to develop models for action are valuable for all institutions.

Smith, D. G. "Diversity." In M. A. Whiteley, J. D. Porter, and R. H. Fenske (eds.), *The Primer for Institutional Research.* Tallahassee, Fla.: Association for Institutional Research, 1992.

This chapter provides a concise description of the types of issues to keep in mind when assessing diversity. It is particularly helpful because it provides both a framework to use in studying diversity and specific questions and techniques to follow. For example, Smith outlines a five-step plan to develop a diversity research study, discusses the existing data sources, and provides specific research questions that could be included in an institutional diversity analysis.

Electronic Mail Lists

The Internet and BITNET are electronic mail networks linking millions of educators (and lots of other people) around the world. One of the features of the networks are mailing lists, subscription lists of people who share common interests. Some of these lists are very active, on others one message a month is the norm. Not all of these lists specialize in discussions of assessment or diversity, and some are not especially active. But queries from interested institutional researchers may create more active lists. Included below are some lists that might be of interest to institutional researchers.

Unless otherwise noted, you subscribe to these lists by sending a one-line message to the LISTSERV address noted. The one line message reads:

Subscribe <name of list> <your name>

You insert the exact name of the list and your real name, and possibly your affiliation. The computer automatically picks up your e-mail address. You "unsubscribe" by sending the command:

Unsub <name of list> or Signoff <name of list>

AFROAM-L, Afro American issues in higher education
    Subscribe to LISTSERV@TEMPLEVM.BITNET
ASHE-L, Association for the Study of Higher Education
    Subscribe to LISTSERV@UMCVMB.BITNET
ASSESS, Assessment in Higher Education
    Subscribe to LISTSERV@UKCC.BITNET
DIVERS-L, Diversity, a new list on diversity in education
    Subscribe to LISTSERV@PSUVM.PSU.EDU
EDAD-L, Educational Administration Discussion list
    Subscribe to LISTSERV@WVNVM.BITNET
EDLAW, Law and education for those who teach and practice law in education settings; a forum for an exchange of information on legislation and litigation
    Subscribe to LISTSERV@UKCC.BITNET
ERL-L, Educational Research List
    Subscribe to LISTSERV@TCSVM.BITNET
L-HCAP, Handicapped People in Education
    Subscribe to LISTSERVE@NDSUVM1.BITNET
NEWEDU-L, New Paradigms in Education
    Subscribe to LISTSERV@USCVM.BITNET

With the following lists, you do not subscribe electronically but ask the list owner to add you to the list. You might also add something about yourself, since you are writing to a person, not a computer. Give your name, e-mail address, affiliation, and so on.

AIR-L, the e-mail list of the Association for Institutional Research, a moderated list; Subscribe by sending message to Larry Nelson,
    NELSON_L@PLU.BITNET
SAO-L, Student Affairs Officers; this list is not moderated, but the list owner adds new members; he is Morton Cotlar,
    MORTON@UNUNIX.UHCC.HAWAII.EDU

This information is correct as of January 1993, but may change before publication.

More information about Internet and BITNET lists is available in the *Internet Companion* (1992) by Tracy LaQuey. More information about lists is available in an e-mail available file, LISTSOFLISTS by Marty Hoag. You can get a copy of this file by sending an e-mail message to LISTSERV@vm1.nodak.edu. The body of the message should include the line GETLISTSOFLISTS. Contact your local computer center for assistance in joining lists.

THOMAS LEVITAN is director of student affairs at the University of South Florida at Sarasota/New College and a doctoral student in higher education at the Claremont Graduate School.

LISA E. WOLF is completing her doctorate in higher education at the Claremont Graduate School and is the residence life coordinator at Scripps College.

INDEX

101

ORDERING INFORMATION

NEW DIRECTIONS FOR INSTITUTIONAL RESEARCH is a series of paperback books that provides planners and administrators in all types of academic institutions with guidelines in such areas as resource coordination, information analysis, program evaluation, and institutional management. Books in the series are published quarterly in spring, summer, fall, and winter and are available for purchase by subscription as well as by single copy.

SUBSCRIPTIONS for 1994 cost $47.00 for individuals (a savings of 25 percent over single-copy prices) and $62.00 for institutions, agencies, and libraries. Please do not send institutional checks for personal subscriptions. Standing orders are accepted.

SINGLE COPIES cost $15.95 when payment accompanies order. (California, New Jersey, New York, and Washington, D.C., residents please include appropriate sales tax.) Billed orders will be charged postage and handling.

DISCOUNTS FOR QUANTITY ORDERS are available. Please write to the address below for information.

ALL ORDERS must include either the name of an individual or an official purchase order number. Please submit your order as follows:
    Subscriptions: specify series and year subscription is to begin
    Single copies: include individual title code (such as IR78)

MAIL ALL ORDERS TO:
    Jossey-Bass Publishers
    350 Sansome Street
    San Francisco, CA 94104-1342

FOR SINGLE-COPY SALES OUTSIDE OF THE UNITED STATES, CONTACT:
    Maxwell Macmillan International Publishing Group
    866 Third Avenue
    New York, NY 10022-6221

FOR SUBSCRIPTION SALES OUTSIDE OF THE UNITED STATES, CONTACT:
    any international subscription agency or Jossey-Bass directly.